WELCOME TO SHANGHAI

歡迎您到上海

A Guide for New Expatriate Residents
to Help Them Make the Most of Their
"Shanghai Experience"

by Tess Johnston

Photographs by Deke Erh

Old China Hand Press
Hong Kong

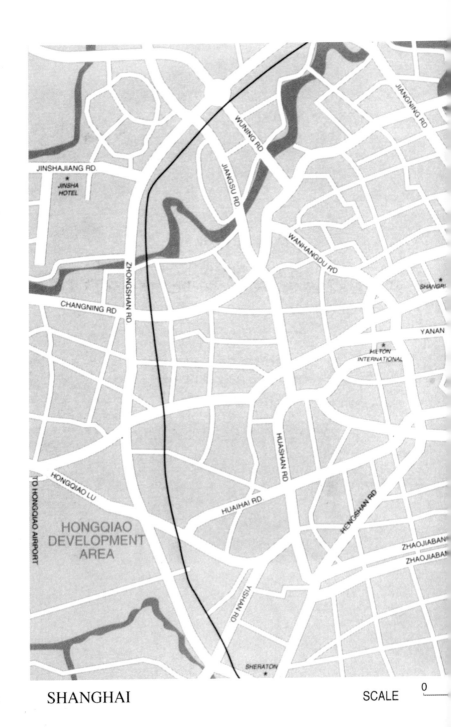

SHANGHAI

SCALE 0

RAIL ———

N

FOREWORD

Whatever may be thought of the judgement of a person who urges foreigners to take the bus in Shanghai, that can make no difference to Tess Johnston. For she is someone who thinks that the gravest danger you run in life is of being bored to death; and what's more she can see what most of us can't, namely a good side to everything. Being crushed beyond belief in a bus crowded enough to reduce most foreigners to a gibbering wreck can no more faze her than put a dent in her good humour.

I am susceptible to her enthusiasm for the city, but then I'm Shanghainese. Others may find it harder to take to the place. How often have I seen a foreigner clutching a beer or a whisky wear that slightly shell-shocked expression common to those newly arrived in Shanghai. Of course you can make it bearable by engaging with it as little as possible, but then you'd be like people who enjoy snow because a plexiglass roof stops it from hitting them.

What Tess gives you in this book are ways of making life not easier but more interesting—not a way out but a way in. What she is saying is that you can dislike nine-tenths of everything that Shanghai offers and still find it rewarding to live there. But for that you'd have to come out of your bubble.

She is the perfect person to write this book not only because she is an aficionado but because she is so knowledgeable. You have only to read her book on Western architecture in Shanghai (*A Last Look*) to recognize this. What you find between its covers is knowledge not just of building styles but of lives lived, of history.

What used to be called Frenchtown (the French Concession of old) is her bailiwick. Though that is not saying much, she knows its streets better than any taxi driver. Legwork and an urge to get cracking have given her unrivalled knowledge of the old neighborhoods and buildings. She knows them all, even—or especially—those mown down to make way for highrises with chandeliers in their marble lobbies. While in search of what she admires she has to look at much which she deplores, but about that she has the gift of being amusing.

Any foreigner who could persuade me that without a ride on the Shanghai bus my life would be incomplete has got to be extraordinary. Tess is. I often forget that she's not native. Yet her secret is actually no secret. You can't study a place for as long as she has and not love it. She is the living demonstration of something I myself have learned through years of expatriation — that the only bonds felt in the heart that we can have with a city or country are those created by things of the mind.

Lynn Pan (Pan Ling)

ACKNOWLEDGMENT

We would like to thank Colliers Jardine Shanghai, who conceived of this project and made this publication possible through their generous support.

TABLE OF CONTENTS

SHANGHAI, A to Z

INTRODUCTION

This relocation guide is designed to help the newcomer get the most out of a Shanghai sojourn, whether it's voluntary or as a hostage to a spouse's employment contract. The subtitle is a double entendre, reflecting a situation not uncommon here where an expatriate has experienced some aggravation that appears to be unique to China (trust us, it's not). This the expats like to call a "Chinese Experience," as in "well, I've just had another Chinese Experience." (And you can be sure that it will later enliven the cocktail circuit.)

Originally this volume was to have had a different title: *Surviving Shanghai — and Loving It.* That is indeed what this book is about but someone else beat us to the title. We are happy, however, to recommend that guide, *Surviving in Shanghai — Where to Find It*, by Sherrie Kline Smith, published by Shanghai's Project HOPE. Not only will you gain useful shopping information from it but buyers of the book, "help Project HOPE bring health and happiness to the children of China through the Shanghai Children's Medical Center." (You may purchase the book at the Business Centre of the Portman Hotel, 1376 Nanjing Xi Lu, or at the Project HOPE office, Tel: 6384-0609.)

Project HOPE's book lists almost everything you might ever want to buy in Shanghai, from "Aquariums" to "Yarn, Knitting" — and where to buy it. It is a Shanghai version of Born to Shop, and we suggest that you use it to supplement this volume. Our book will give you the big picture, some armchair philosophizing and the petty details, and theirs will show you where and how to shop in Shanghai.

The author of this guidebook is uniquely qualified to share Shanghai with you; she has been here since 1981 and professes to have enjoyed every minute of it. Armed with nothing more than an open mind and basic Mandarin Chinese, and while putting in a full work week, she managed nonetheless to become a renowned research resource and to author, along with her partner Deke Erh (whose photographs enliven this book), five volumes on Western architecture in China.

Here the author shares with you what she has learned over her years in Shanghai along with some of the resources she has found most useful. She hopes to give you some ideas and maybe even to inspire you — all with the aim of making both fun and fruitful your "Shanghai Experience."

Enjoy!

Chapter ❶

SHANGHAI'S HISTORY

We'll run through the boring stuff fast. On the Whangpoo River, a tributary of the Yangtze, there was this little fishing village called "Hu" with walls dating back to the Ming Dynasty (memorize that one, 1368-1644). The city grew and grew and, as you guessed, ultimately became the metropolis of Shanghai with thirteen million inhabitants — and still growing.

It was not only a fishing port but was also a natural gateway to China's interior. In the mid-19th century the foreigners realized the significance of the latter. When the British won the so-called First Opium War in 1843 they forced the Chinese to sign treaties that opened Shanghai and four other ports to Western trade. By the 1860's the city was booming. The small foreign population was soon overwhelmed by half a million Chinese fleeing for protection to the settlement from two rebellions that were devastating the surrounding countryside.

This influx was not all bad news if you happened to be in real estate. The subsequent scramble for prime property saw downtown land lease prices rise a thousand fold — and since then they have risen a million fold. Along with the lucrative opium trade land speculation was the basis for many a fortune of Shanghai's "first families."

There were actually four Shanghais then: the American, north of Suzhou Creek; the British, around the Bund; the French, to the south and west; and the walled "native city" of the Chinese, whose egg shape is still clearly discernible on Shanghai maps. The Americans and Brits soon agreed to merge as the International Settlement while the French chose to go it alone as a separate concession, which quickly became known as "Frenchtown." Only the native city was beyond the pale for foreigners, who were advised to enter it only with an armed escort.

The foreigners' idea was to keep their settlements for themselves but that didn't last long. The wealthier Chinese preferred the comparative safety, law and order offered by the settlements to that of their own walled enclave and city's segregation soon crumbled in the face of offers that the foreigners could not refuse. After that it was Boomtown Shanghai.

As with its counterparts in the Western world in Shanghai too prostitution, opium and gambling soon flourished. In 1864 the British consul claimed that of the ten thousand Chinese residences in the foreign settlements 668 were brothels. (The Chinese have always been quick off the mark to spot a business opportunity.) Shanghai thus very early earned its reputation as "the wickedest city in the East," a reputation that ended only under the puritanical communist regime in the early 1950's.

Between the world wars there sprang up in Shanghai many of the buildings you see today, or rather, you see vanishing today. It was the great age of great buildings: the Bund's banking houses, Nanking Road's four dominant department stores, the elegant club houses of the major nations, the magnificent mansions in the French Concession, the Art Deco skyscrapers and cinemas everywhere. You could write whole books about them (and we have).

Throughout the twenties and thirties Shanghai continued to prosper, to work and to play with equal vigor through the wars and upheavals that swirled around her. If anything these fostered the *fin du siecle* gaiety that had always been a hallmark of the city. Only when the Japanese forces marched into the foreign settlements on December 8, 1941, did the city settle into an uneasy slumber that lasted for many years.

In 1942 the foreigners of the Allied powers were interned. In 1943 the Jewish refugees, who had fled from Hitler's Europe to a wide-open Shanghai, were forced into a ghetto in Hongkou, the devastated area north of Suzhou Creek. Shanghai was no longer an international city, one of foreigners' privilege and power. For the first time the Chinese and the foreigners all suffered alike.

After the war ended the newly released foreign businessmen tried to restart their businesses and resume their former role in Shanghai. The Chinese had seen, however, that the white man could be bested by the Asian and that was the beginning of the end for the foreigners in China. The more prescient among them saw the handwriting on the wall and the exodus of the Westerners began. When the Communists marched into the city in 1949 that put paid to the foreigners' power there. Within five years, and for the first time in nearly a hundred years, Shanghai became a purely Chinese city.

The city is once again an international one and the foreigners are back in full force. As one of them you are in a unique position to watch Shanghai try to recapture its former glory. It appears to be well on the way. There is no place in the world that is undergoing such rapid and exciting social change. (Your author has seen the city come up about a century in the last decade.) As a new Shanghai resident you are fortunate in being in the right place and at the right time to see history being made.

Here we've hit only the historical high spots to whet your appetite. We urge you to do your homework, to read up on Shanghai's colorful history. It will help you to better understand the city in which you will be living. It can also form the basis for fascinating further exploration.

Chapter 2

WHY AM I HERE — AND WHAT AM I GOING TO DO ABOUT IT?

In part your Shanghai Experience will depend on the answer to these questions. If you are here as a businessperson, assigned to a job that will supply an environment rich in challenges as well as knowledgeable and helpful (we hope) personnel then your outlook will be entirely different from that of a house-bound spouse. She (or possibly he) will in most cases initially have the companionship only of a few neighbors, if lucky, and the ubiquitous ayi or housekeeper (we use the term loosely here) who speaks no known language.

The children can quickly escape to the excitement of a new school but the only escape you can count on is the one you create for yourself. If you are going to live a full, happy and productive life in Shanghai you are going to have to find something that grabs you. China, and most especially Shanghai, is rich in many things but finding the one that best suits your situation and personality is the challenge. That's why we wrote this book — to help you do just that. In Chapter Five we give you ten possible ways to go and then in Chapter Six we give you personal accounts of people who have gone those routes and how it all turned out.

The first thing you've got to do is to get over what the social scientists like to call "Culture Shock." (This is not a phenomenon unique to China; your author experiences

it in New York City, to say nothing of California.) You are initially going to see the city in a totally different light from the Shanghainese. To quote from a briefing paper of the American Consulate General:

"With its vast range of cultural, intellectual, entertainment and recreational opportunities, as well as its unmistakable big-city feel, Shanghai is an exciting place to live. There is a universal assumption that, with a few obvious exceptions like housing, things are always better in Shanghai. Finally, the Shanghainese share with New Yorkers and Londoners an inability to imagine truly living anywhere else."

Shanghainese (and the author) may think their city is nifty but your initial impression may well be that nothing works and nobody cares. This will gradually change to amazement that anything works at all, but somehow it does. You peer out your window into a pall of pollution that is reminiscent, or so our Pittsburgh friends tell us, of that city in the 1930's. Downtown traffic is gridlocked even at midnight. This doesn't matter as few taxi drivers can ever take you where you want to go anyway — even if they know the location, which is doubtful. (Local wits say "if you're a stranger in Shanghai take a taxi — that'll make two strangers.")

As for the motorcycles and mopeds, they are most often on the sidewalks, going against traffic of course, along with about ten million bicycles. As the "Right on Red" rule applies here, crossing the street — even with a green WALK signal staring you in the face — is a death-defying act. Ah yes, those sidewalks. You can never walk with your eyes on the stars or you will fall into one of Shanghai's ubiquitous unprotected openings. The streets always seem to be torn up for something or other and manhole covers are routinely stolen for their scrap metal value.

An even more fearsome hazard is the vigorous clearing of nasal passages and the results thereof, to put a more delicate spin on it; they're awe-inspiring if not terrifying. (This author can recall, however, when spittoons were also very much in evidence in the United States; granted it has been a while.)

Some days you may ask yourself, what is a nice gal/guy like me doing here anyway? You just want to go back to bed and cover up your head until it's time to go home. No no no. Some days it may take an act of faith to do so but you must hit the streets. There's life out there, life described by Aldous Huxley as "dense, richly clotted life...Old Shanghai is elan vital in the raw, so to speak, and with the lid off. It is Life itself."

We grant that you probably will not find your initial impression one of dazzled bewonderment. Despite what the Shanghainese may think, and despite its former sobriquet "Paris of the Orient," Paris it is not. (But you should know that your author once curtailed a tour in Paris to return to Shanghai, thus making everything she writes here highly suspect.) If you can find no other motivation to explore the city and its environs then think upon your excursions as sociological studies.

In passing the author would like to report that she, once a sheltered Southern lady, ultimately evolved to the point where she could bicycle through the crowded and certainly clotted alleys of Old Town, with clothes dripping on her head and life pulsing and throbbing all around her, and invariably find that she was smiling throughout. You may never get to quite that point (although we hope you do) but trust us you will never, ever, be bored by the life on Shanghai's streets.

Must you leave your lovely home, your new expatriate friends? Of course not; we do have choices even in Shanghai. Here your author has distilled them down to three and given them labels. We like to keep it simple, to get you pigeon-holed and then we can move on from there.

Choice One: The Gilded Cage.

There are ten five-star hotels and probably ten times as many first-class restaurants in Shanghai. There are Western-style super-markets, drug stores and department stores (and we give you a long list at the back of this book) plus plenty of pricey boutiques with all the designer labels you can possibly afford. Every major hotel has a delicatessen and the city boasts numerous American fast food franchises (but all somehow have "Chinese characteristics").

There are "expatriates only" associations just as there have always been in Shanghai. In short, you can surround yourself with your native things and confine your friendships to your own kind and you'll never have to set foot in the China of the Chinese. Some expats never do — and then return home to boast of their vast China experience.

Choice Two: Modified "Mixing with the Masses" (or MMM).

MMM is the middle road. No *da bizi* ("big nose," the non-pejorative nomenclature given to Westerners here) can ever really mix with the masses; our faces give us away and we remain ever the *waiguoren* or "outside people." (If you are of Asian origin then you will have a whole different set of problems, which our Asian friends tell us are equally excluding.) But even as "Shanghailanders" (who landed here, get it?) we can still share some of the trials and triumphs, the joys and sorrows, the customs and ceremonies of the local Shanghainese.

To go this route is not easy. First you must have at least a smattering of conversational Chinese, which is a real undertaking. Unless you are Asian or a demi-genius you may as well forget trying to learn to read and write; you're probably not going to live long enough to accomplish that miracle. (Ask the author; she's been studying Mandarin off and on for over a decade with miserably meager results.)

Secondly, you are not permitted to become a hired-car habitué. You must commit yourself to walking, riding a bicycle or taking local busses, albeit not during rush hours — that would be asking too much of you. Or there is always the new subway, which is considerably cleaner than ours in the USA we might add. You will shop in local shops, go to local cinemas and concerts, eat in holes-in-the-walls or — oh horror — from street stalls. (Never mind, your stomach will adapt and you probably won't die of it; a billion-plus Chinese haven't.)

Of course you must have Chinese friends and that's the hard part. We will cover this thorny problem later in more detail. Friends are usually found in the workplace so if you don't work outside the home you lose a valuable source for contacts. An open mind and a friendly smile will do wonders in easing the irritations of MMM but it probably won't net you any Chinese friends, with the possible exception of those with hidden agendas (and more on this also later).

What MMM will give you is an insight into how the Chinese live and armed with this valuable knowledge, not always sought out or appreciated by Westerners, you at least have a head start in what can amount to a lifelong attempt to understand China. It's an education for which you would pay megabucks in a university back home and here you have a chance to pick up container-loads relatively free. Oy vey such a deal.

Choice Three: Going Native.

This represents the far end of the spectrum and is easy for Western students at Chinese universities, where they can meet and date the Chinese (and thus acquire those enviable "walking dictionaries" we all so need). It is also possible for the older expat and perhaps a little easier for males than females. (Incidentally for what it's worth, the Shanghainese slang for foreigners who date Chinese is *feijipiao* or "airline ticket.")

Some young businessmen and women, who jokingly call themselves "Shanghai Geeks," have managed to live in local housing in the lanes —the *ne plus ultra* in expat housing for the young or young-at-heart — and to hang out almost exclusively with Chinese friends. Needless to say their language skills are enviable and in such an environment improve by the cube of the word, unlike those of the expats who

must spend their days inundated only in English or some European language.

Granted Choice Three is not an option for all and it takes a certain creativity and hardihood to go this route; a Chinese life is not an easy one. (There's the plumbing, for starters.) As the Geeks will tell you, however, they feel the reward worth the effort. After all, you can always write a book about your experiences. (Mark Salzman immediately comes to mind as the ultimate China Geek; his *Iron and Silk* is an engrossing account of his mastery of an arcane martial arts technique.)

There is an incredibly rich and varied stratum of culture among the Chinese artists, writers and intellectuals (scratch almost any Shanghainese and you find an intellectual). If you are persistent or fortunate enough to be accepted in such a milieu then you've got it made. Geeks wind up staying out here for years and years (your author among them). Furthermore your future is assured: When you do go home a prestigious university or think tank will probably want to hire you as a "China expert" (not usually an ill-paid sinecure we might add). Go Native if you really want to learn how China works.

In subsequent chapters we will try to refine your choices even further for you.

Chapter 3

A GLIMPSE BEHIND THE CHINESE SCREEN

In the previous chapter we mentioned a few of the problems you will probably encounter. Although by no means an expert on China, your author in her sixteen years here has learned a few things about the How's and Why's of the country that she would like to share with you.

Let's start with a few key words. One concept that you will encounter frequently and without which China could not function is *guanxi* (pronounced gwan-shee). This is best translated by the English word "connections" but it goes beyond that. It is an interlocking set of favors and obligations that is the grease that keeps the wheels turning. For example an introduction to a good English tutor in return for assistance in obtaining a fast telephone hook-up — like trading pigs for grain.

In your own country public services are, theoretically at least, rendered to the public openly and impartially. You need a driver's license so you study, you take your test, you pass and you get your license. Although some Western systems are complicated (and some possibly corrupt) the public services fulfill their function and you get what they are supposed to give you.

In China the system is more complicated and opaque. The services are there all right but threading your way through the maze and coming out at the end with what you seek is not necessarily going to happen. The cumbersome bureaucracy moves slowly, it doesn't function efficiently and the functionaries appear uninterested in seeing it do so unless there is something in it for them personally.

This is where *guanxi* comes in. If the supplicant knows someone who works in that office, or knows someone who knows someone, then he or she gets in touch with that person and sees if the *guanxi* can be brought into play. This of course means that the persons who helped will automatically be helped by return *guanxi* at some future time when they need it.

The blank check is out and you may rest assured that someday it will be cashed. That is why you husband your *guanxi* carefully and bestow it on the most deserving or the most valuable recipient; you don't want to squander your stockpile. Everyone seems to have something to trade off and if not then a gift would be expected. Of course a discreet gift in the office involved might also work and might in the long run be cheaper, but as a foreigner we assume you wouldn't know how or whom to bribe.

If you have a business affiliation here then you will in most cases have ample assistance from your or your spouse's office or work unit to help you run the bureaucratic gauntlets — which is fortunate as both *guanxi* and the gift giving ritual are bit of an acquired art.

The gift giving and receiving alone is a tricky business in China. As a foreigner you are perceived to have much to offer. Your new Chinese friend or acquaintance needs a college scholarship for a relative or financial sponsorship or (the blight of our lives here) simply assumes you have access to the nice folks at your consulate and can assist in getting the needed visa or even in overturning a recent refusal of one.

Perhaps you do have that access but in all the visa sections that we know of visas are adjudicated on merit. A "good word" by a Western friend, passed on in private to your friend at the Consulate General, might help in some cases; we don't know. We do know that attempting to breach the visa line in order to assist your Chinese friend will probably earn you a polite request to leave, as only the applicants themselves are generally allowed at the visa window. (For your or your spouse's office personnel there are different avenues to pursue for business visas and you need not get personally involved in them.)

If the person requesting your help is a truly good friend, as opposed to an opportunistic recent acquaintance, you may wish to help in some way. The easiest way, assuming you are not loaded with consular officer friends, would be to write a fulsome letter in support of the applicant. (Not to be confused with the "Affidavit of Support" that promises financial support; that is usually done on a special form and requires that you also supply personal financial data to back up your support.) The letter may or may not do any good but at least you will have shown that you care and that you tried.

Now back to this gift giving problem. The Chinese lay great ceremony on ceremony and they will invariably present you with little gifts (we hope only little ones) if they are invited to your home or over the Chinese holidays or for some special occasion. These you will want to accept, and with both hands (in order not to appear ungrateful). You thank them and then promptly set the gift aside and do not refer to it again. You will note that this is how the Chinese do it. To gush and rave over a gift as we often do in Western countries (most especially if it is truly a Great Gift) smacks to the Chinese of materialism, or at least of insincerity.

But suppose you hardly know someone and they present you with a Great Gift, something that appears expensive or at least well beyond their means? These are those acquaintances with "hidden agendas" that we mentioned earlier. This sort of gift you must politely but firmly refuse because it will most surely be followed fairly soon by a request for some assistance that you may be unwilling or unable to provide (such as that visa). You certainly don't want to be beholden to a mere acquaintance so that it makes it awkward to refuse a request. Even at the risk of being rude you must refuse significant gifts from people you hardly know. That is virtually the only time you will be allowed to refuse so enjoy the moment.

About that gushing and raving. If you are invited into a Chinese home or if you become friends with artists or artisans and you spot something that enchants you by all means pay a compliment — but watch out. If you are too enthusiastic the poor host or artist or artisan will be obliged to offer the object to you as a gift. Your job then is to wiggle out of accepting the gift without offending the giver. It is much better not to set yourself up for such a chore in the first place. (For more details on gift giving etiquette, see Category G in *Shanghai, from A to Z,* an appendix to this book.)

We hope that you will develop a network of Chinese friends with whom you can just be yourself, behave as you like. Since we assume that you do not yet speak Chinese well your friends probably are those who speak a Western language and hence may have a more "open" and Western outlook. Initially, however, you had better play by the basic Chinese rules and restrain yourself a bit, at least until you get the feel of the friendship and are on solid ground.

Quite often your first friends will come from your or your spouse's workplace. These, however, will be formal ones and the entertaining will be more stylized, almost always involving banquets in local restaurants. Here you must always reciprocate in kind. You will need to be very protocol-conscious in the beginning stages so turn to your Chinese office staff for suggestions.

A word of warning: We Westerners love to discover little hole-in-the-wall restaurants on back streets and to share them with our Western friends. To take Chinese guests there only makes them think you are cheap. They like the glitter and glitz and cannot comprehend that you would choose any less. So save the little ethnic restaurants for your Western friends and give the Chinese what they love and expect, including of course lots of rare delicacies like the dreaded sea slug, the scourge of Western palates.

You surely would not have come to China without knowing the significance of food in Chinese life. The millions of Chinese eateries abroad should have taught you something. It is their life. Over fifty percent of the Shanghainese income goes toward food (so it's fortunate that the local rents and rates are low). Remember there have been many cycles in Chinese history where the populace has starved and there are still people in China who do not have much to eat. The Chinese never forget this.

Every special event, large or small, is an occasion that calls for dining out or at home with some special delicacies. If you are fortunate enough to be invited into a Chinese home do not expect to see much of the hostess; she will be in the kitchen either cooking or supervising (if she is lucky enough to have an ayi). She may make cameo appearances at the table but her first obligation is to present her guests with delicious food; her husband and family will be expected to handle the protocol at the table.

We might add that there is no greater honor than to be invited to dine in a Chinese home and you are expected to accept the invitation. Once you have done so you must never, ever, except in the most dire emergencies cancel out. The hosts will have spent days planning the menu and stockpiling the goodies and they will probably have alerted their neighbors of your impending visit. For the guests not to show up is unthinkable. That would represent a real loss of "Face."

Ah yes, this matter of Face, after *guanxi* the second most important concept to master in the Chinese mosaic. It is perhaps even more important than *guanxi*, which is after all only a means of getting things done. Face is the very core of one's existence. You can give Face to the Chinese or you can take it away from them through some action. The latter is hitting them where they live.

This is not an unknown concept in the West, where we have the widely understood term "to lose face." It means there what it means here: to rob someone, in their eyes, of their dignity or their worth. Unfortunately we in the West are not always sensitized as to what constitutes making someone lose Face in China. The obvious things like berating people in public, bluntly doubting their wisdom or scorning their suggestions, almost anything negative that you say or do to a Chinese that is done in public will make them lose Face.

It is therefore best to restrain any criticism of colleagues, employees or servants to

a private moment and even then to put a tactful spin on it, such as saying "in our country we think that..." or some formula to make the recipient feel a little less put upon. You can always say "There has been a misunderstanding..." — because there usually has been. He or she may not like it or even understand your criticism but at least it wasn't done in public. Indeed, the cultural differences between China and the Western world are so great that often the recipients of your ire may be deeply offended, not perceiving that they did anything wrong (obviously we are not talking here of gross malfeasance).

To "Give Face" you need not be a high-ranking official or movie star although of course that helps. Your own Western face may sometimes suffice. If your favorite restaurant has a grand event and you are invited the owner will probably place you in a prominent position, especially if he is hoping to court a Western clientele.

At gallery openings, musical events or any galas put on by the Chinese the Westerners are almost always right up front. China now has a policy of "opening to the west" and it is very much a la mode to have Western clientele, customers and friends. Aren't we lucky? Just by virtue of our smiling Western faces and just standing there breathing we can sometimes grant Face to friends and their establishments.

About those cultural differences: Where to start? Thick tomes have been written about them, seminars held, classes taught. We suggest you try any or all three of these offerings if you really want to get a handle on China's culture. We will only mention in passing some of the most important aspects, starting with family.

In China family is everything and a man who has no family is considered, no matter what his wealth or fame, a poor creature indeed. First you take care of your family then your close friends and then your fellow man, the latter in very distant third place. This partially accounts for a certain civic indifference that has for centuries characterized China.

If a Chinese does not aid a man injured or dying on the street it is not necessarily that he or she is totally unmoved by that person's plight. Even in more advanced Western countries unwillingness to get involved is not unknown; newspapers abound in horror stories of civic indifference in the West's most prosperous cities. For the Chinese to get involved in something that does not concern them can only bring all sorts of unwelcome complications and responsibilities. This is after all the country where until not too long ago if you saved a person's life you "owned" that person for as long as he or she might live. The rationale was that you had diverted a destiny and now he or she was your responsibility.

In some Asian countries to resist a bribe or not to avail oneself of some corrupt but lucrative offer is thought to be unfair to the family, denying them a chance to better themselves at the expense of a remote and impersonal state. (The Chinese have a saying, "heaven is high and the Emperor far away".) One's family is right here and is one's immediate responsibility. Whether this philosophy still holds true in China we do not know; it is a murky area we have not explored.

Is it social indifference that makes queuing up in China — an oxymoron if there ever was one — almost unheard of? As you will note early in your sojourn here lines seem to form horizontally rather than vertically. You may be the first person at the kiosk window but unless you are particularly adept with the elbows you most certainly will not be the first person served. The concept of first-come-first-served is, to say the least, not highly developed in China.

In the West the Anglo-Saxon sense of "fair play" is deeply ingrained. It is easy to play fair in a line if everyone else does and if there is reason to believe that the distribution at the front end of the line will be equitable and sufficient. In China neither of these factors is a given and if you do not get in there and fight for it there is a good chance that nothing will be left when you finally make it to the front. (Remember, a portion of any popular product will already have been skimmed off behind the scenes to sell to friends or exchange for *guanxi*.)

In a country of a billion-plus population there is never enough of everything for everybody, as the Chinese are well aware. You may try shaming them with a few neat phrases like "I believe I was here first" but we have never found that this works. The Chinese only wonder why we are standing by so passively in line if it is something we really want. You will never get used to it and it will never cease to irritate you but you better relax and learn to live with it. You are never going to change Chinese line-standing etiquette so save your effort. You can always have your ayi do it if it really does you in.

A word about that. Remember our discussion of Face? When it is something that is really important the ayi will perhaps ask her Western employer to go with her. Just the presence of a Western face alongside hers will guarantee her a modicum of attention, that little extra push that may help to get the coveted item. She will do the work but you have to be standing with her so that she can launch into her story about how the foreign friend needs, wants, longs for this item. If it is something for your benefit you can cooperate or not as you choose; if it is something for her benefit we trust you will always be willing to lend a hand — or a face.

By the way, did you know that your ayi will not be able to get good treatment in a hospital, to get a needed operation scheduled, to get a good doctor, to get almost anything without either a gift or *guanxi* (and she may not have much to offer in return, so may not be loaded with it). Corruption has reached down to the most basic level of China's economy and is hitting the little man (called *lao bai xing* or "old hundred names") where it hurts, literally: in medical services. Keep that in mind. You may want to offer your face some day to help your ayi or your Chinese friends stay healthy.

One last word about Chinese "*keqi*" or formalized politeness. Custom demands that the Chinese be overly so and to the denigration of themselves. The days are not long past when such phrases as "my unworthy name" were used and the Chinese must still vigorously maintain that they are not worthy of the honor or compliments bestowed upon them. The older and more cultured the speaker the more this sort of disclaimer will be used. The younger generation is, however, just as heedless and rude as anywhere else in the world. Perhaps more so now that China is a country of spoiled "only children."

As a Westerner anything you do is praised to the skies. Where else in the world can your halting and badly accented "*Ni Hao*" cause the listeners to gasp in admiration of your Chinese language capability? (Using her French the author certainly never had that effect on the Parisians.) All the more reason for you to learn Chinese; even your most infantile utterances are appreciated, if not greeted with downright delight. You must of course always deny that you speak Chinese well. (That should be easy as you probably don't.) Try saying, "*nali nali*" (rhymes with the American pronunciation of polly-wolly) while tugging at the forelock.

If you wish to show your cultural sensitivity you must always disclaim modestly any compliment paid you, and must never make the mistake that the author once did of saying "Come up to my penthouse and see my lovely view." Remember, nothing you have or create or do is lovely; it is only a poor effort, a small thing unworthy of praise.

Do the Chinese believe this? Of course not, not on their side and not on yours. Being a Westerner, if you like brutal honesty then you don't have to do this false modesty bit at all; after all, you did this wonderful thing and of course you deserve the praise. If you do choose to follow the Chinese custom, however, the Chinese will know that you took the time to learn something about their culture and they will appreciate it. It elevates you a bit in their eyes — and we Westerners need all the help we can get in this alien land.

There are a million and one little subtleties in Chinese life and with effort you may learn a few. (To help you we have included some more in our *Shanghai, from A to Z* at the back of this book.) If you are not of Chinese origin, or even if you are but are one generation removed from China, you will never be able to peer very far below the surface of Chinese life. The most you can hope for is brief glimpses, a few little flashes of insight — aha, so that's what that was all about.

Finding out the real meaning behind the words takes talent, a good grasp of psychology and most of all a deep understanding of the Chinese mentality. Many Western businessmen negotiating contracts with the Chinese have thought they had it down pat. You just say your piece up front, lay your cards on the table, the other side does the same and you wind it up. Only much later and to their consternation do they find out that what is said and what is meant, at least on the Chinese side, are two different things.

Western businessmen maintain that the Chinese don't begin the real negotiations until after the contract is signed. Incidentally, we have never heard of a Western businessman besting a Chinese in contract talks. The Westerners finally give away the store — only to find out that what the Chinese really want is the whole square block.

We are not here, however, to discuss such an arcane subject as negotiating with the Chinese; we wouldn't touch that topic with a barge pole. In any event numerous books have been written on this subject and if you intend to engage in business in China you must study them assiduously. What we are trying to show you is that what's up front and what's behind it here are not necessarily the same thing. (Are they anywhere, for that matter?) You need not necessarily believe everything you hear in China. And certainly not what you read in their newspapers. (Even the Chinese get most of their information by reading between the lines.)

Your ayi's grandmother died and she must return to her village? Of course she must go (as she will anyway) and you may want to advance her a little money for the trip. Only after you get to her third or fourth grandmother do you begin to think maybe something is fishy. Oh, she didn't come back, sent a message that she had to stay home with the distraught family? Perhaps that is true. But perhaps you've lost an ayi who didn't want to tell you that she didn't like you, your style, your working conditions, your salary level, or whatever it was.

Who likes confrontations anyway? (Certainly not your author; maybe that's why she gets along so well in China.) Here you didn't have one and both you and the ayi saved face. Incidentally, we do hope that if you spot your errant ayi again, perhaps working for a neighbor, you are a class act and graciously greet her. (But who among us could resist the temptation to inquire sweetly about the health of her bereaved family? We certainly couldn't.)

There are some things in China that we will never understand. Why buy a play or concert ticket and then talk at full conversational level (while eating candy out of a crackly bag) throughout? Why try to enter a jammed bus exit while everyone is trying to get off, thus defeating your purpose. Why halt your car (or bicycle or moped or motorcycle) right in the middle of a busy street, forcing others to maneuver slowly around you or, better yet, stop completely, horns blaring, until you solve your problem? (Listen, we've seen bike repairs accomplished in the semi-middle of a busy street!) Why why why.

Your author once queried a harassed and hostile Chinese functionary why ("*wei shema*"?) he had done something that appeared to be counterproductive to the situation. His irate reply: "*meiyou wei shema.*" There is no "why." That about sums it up.

Although China has (in theory anyway) a classless society it is important to distinguish between the actions of the educated Mandarin class and that of peasants just in from the countryside. Their behavior will be no more alike than that of a Boston Brahmin and a redneck "good ole boy" in the United States.

The worst manifestations of bad behavior, of breaking the highly complex set of rules that form the Chinese culture and govern Chinese civilization, you would expect to occur among the uneducated peasant classes. As millions of peasants swarm to Shanghai to work in the construction industry they are an easy —and by far the favorite — target. But our experience has been that the peasant lads can be touchingly polite and helpful and it's the big city louts and lay-abouts who are the most rude and crude. Anyway it's not your problem so save your breath and don't take it upon yourself to try to teach any miscreant anything; leave that to their fellow countrymen. You've got enough problems just teaching yourself.

Even an undereducated or illiterate peasant lives by a code of rules that is the backbone of Chinese society — or used to be: respect for the aged, taking care of

one's own family, paying homage to one's ancestors, and other fine points we have discussed. It is only in the area of civic responsibility that he falls far short. And that is, alas, the area most visible to the foreigners.

But back to the class from which your friends will be drawn.

Among the educated true emotions are almost never revealed. This is partly for self-protection. (There was once in Mao's China a campaign called "Let a Hundred Flowers Bloom." Ask your Chinese friends some day about the perils of offering constructive criticism or "blooming" too early.) This reticence is also part of the Chinese culture. To reveal anger or acute distress, to form instant "friendships" even with those puppy-friendly foreigners, to open your home and your family circle to strangers, to reveal anything to anyone not close to you, this is deemed not wise. (At least you're not burdened with Chinese seat mates on airplanes telling you their entire marital history.)

Watch two Chinese standing side by side interact with each other at a social function. They will hardly speak, or will make only the most inane conversation (don't we all?), unless and until they find they went to the same school or perhaps come from the same *lao jia* (native place). Now they are on safe ground among their own and can be a little more trusting. The conversation will warm up considerably.

Your author, blessed with a large circle of Chinese friends, once had a cocktail party that was attended by two of her close friends. They were correct but distant with each other until the hostess happened to mention to one that the other was a also a graduate of St. John's (Shanghai's Harvard), albeit of a much earlier year. A lively exchange ensued and soon a few other old Johanneans joined in. It turned out that most of these people, who had known the author for years and had seen each other not infrequently at her home, had never discovered that they had a common bond other than the author herself.

Now several of them have become friends with each other. This probably would never have happened had the author not introduced the St. John's element into the conversation, thus making them feel comfortable enough to open up a bit. In America this would never happen. There it is joked that if a person is from either Harvard or Texas he will interject that fact into the first three minutes of any conversation; you'd be surprised how often this proves true. Watch Chinese at any social event. It is a fascinating study of interaction, or lack of it. (Because they are around Westerners, however, our friends may be a bit more outgoing than is traditional, thus invalidating our point.)

Wait a minute, the Chinese don't show anger? We can hear you protesting already. How about those fist fights you see, the screaming matches between taxi drivers or even between two old ladies on the street — you call that restraint? First of all we said the educated classes. Secondly this is New

China emerging and the rules of the game are changing about as fast as the country is changing, and that is with alarming speed. The up side is that young people are becoming more open to new ideas, in fact seem to be obsessed by Western ideas, music, trademarks, possessions.

The down side is that these rapid social changes are tearing apart the fabric of society and creating confusion and stress. People seem increasingly to be adrift as all the old values, the job security, the "iron rice bowl" and other perks, disappear and they cannot see clearly what is to replace them (nor can we, for that matter).

As the Chinese seek something to hold on to the younger and more affluent are turning to the West or toward conspicuous consumption — and often both. What else would account for a pretty young thing at a recent concert of Western music having to leave her seat three times during one movement to take telephone calls on her mobile phone? Of course she could have been a brain surgeon on call, or perhaps a busy call girl, who knows? For one thing she had a "*dageda*" (or "Dial Big Brother" as mobile phones are called here) and that was more than we did; we had only the music to listen to. If you have it flaunt it. The current jet set in Shanghai is giving a whole new dimension to the characteristics we associate with the *nouveaux riches* of the West.

Other and less privileged Chinese are turning to the Christian religion as well as to the teachings of Confucius, and the churches and temples are overflowing. Some seek to travel abroad for the first time in their lives and the visa lines are overflowing. (Did you know that 7% of all American immigrants come from China?) All are longing and striving to share in Shanghai's new prosperity but it eludes many and the gap between the rich and the poor grows wider. This means further worry and stress for the average Chinese citizen, and gives the Chinese government cause for concern.

We have dealt on the lofty plain of theory when discussing Chinese customs and traditions and how they affect you. The reality of daily life in Shanghai may be something entirely different. Your author always lives in the past so perhaps she is totally out of touch and none of this formalized behavior is to be found anymore in the circles in which you will move. Perhaps it is practiced and appreciated only by ancients like herself.

In any event, consider it historical background information if nothing else. Our advice, however (and that's what you bought this book for), is still this: Realize that you don't have a clue as to what's really going on and then err on the side of the conservative approach —that's the way to err, if indeed you must. Of course we would rather that you grasp instinctively what China is all about (we wish you luck!) and not err too often. Lord knows we try.

But cheer up, you will always be forgiven even your most awful goofs; after all as a foreigner how could you possibly know any better? That is why it will pay you to do some homework and learn about some of the fascinating things that go on beneath the surface of Chinese life. You can surprise them.

Chapter 4

NUTS AND BOLTS

There are certain things you need to live in Shanghai. The first and foremost is of course a place to live. Some companies send their employees and spouses out on a preliminary trip to scout things out. This would help you to get a leg up so to speak but it is not necessary if you are willing to live in a hotel for a while.

The good news is that the "while" is a great deal shorter than it used to be. Several years ago the housing situation for foreigners in Shanghai was a sellers' market in every sense of the word and the prices reflected that — sky high! In 1996-97 thousands of new houses and apartment blocks were completed and this radically changed the picture, much to the relief of Shanghai's expatriate community.

As of this writing real estate prices are still dropping and the range of offerings is expanding exponentially. Where previously there was only one villa complex considered to be up to Western standards now there are scores. New apartment complexes abound and with every new building that comes on line a new real estate company appears on the scene to flog it. There are now hundreds of real estate offices and agencies, ranging from some pretty dodgy ones to the well-known international companies.

Whether you choose to use one is up to you but you should be aware that it is not always the owner alone who pays the finders' fees. Often both the owner and the tenant pay equally. If you do decide to use an agent ask around and get recommendations from other expats or your office staff; everyone knows at least one real estate agent.

Many joint ventures have already purchased or leased property for their expat employees, who can move right in when they arrive. This certainly simplifies things but of course their choice may not necessarily be what you would have chosen.

A quick run-down of the choices:

(1) New full-service villas. These are fully furnished, right down to linens and dinnerware, and provide all services, including housecleaning, gardening and maintenance. There are always sports facilities and a fitness center, a club house, a restaurant, shuttle busses into town, in short everything you need to live a life of ease and (hopefully) elegance. This cosseting is a fairly new concept on the Shanghai scene and is very popular. It is also very pricey.

(2) New villas. These you rent just as you would a house back in your native country. Here you supply your own ayi, you are sometimes responsible for the upkeep and although there is usually a shuttlebus service it is often not frequent and sometimes unreliable. There are probably sports facilities and club houses, the range of offerings varying greatly. These villa complexes abound in Shanghai's suburbs and smaller ones are beginning to appear in the more sought-after locations in town such as Shanghai's old French Concession. The good news is that rental prices have recently dropped below ten thousand (yes, that's U.S. dollars) a month. The bad news is that the new buildings are almost invariably sheathed in lavatorial tiling, not the most attractive of exterior finishes to say the least. If it's real class you are after then you will want to go for:

(3) The older villas. Much sought after, they are generally located nearer the center of the city and were generally built in the 1920's-1940's. They can be charming and often have a garden and a garage. They can also be fraught with problems, everything from creeping ground damp and mildew to lack of enough electrical current to run all the appliances. (Do you really want to turn off your air conditioner in order to toast your bread?) Everything depends on the quality of the renovation. The better ones have taken all these problems into account but rental prices reflect the expenses

involved. For many (including the author), however, this is the only way to go.

(4) The lane housing. Lanes shoot off in every direction from the major thoroughfares in Shanghai and once you get away from the busy streets you are in an entirely different world, one of calm and

quiet. (Granted, the latter depends somewhat on the nature of the lane and the sophistication of its inhabitants.) Villas or duplexes line both sides of the lane and sometimes there are small apartment houses tucked away at the far end. In the lanes you will sacrifice a bit of privacy, as your comings and goings will always be noted with interest, but you do get to know your neighbors. During the day they will consist of mostly grannies and their charges; everyone else is at work. Here you have a real sense of community and you are truly living in China.

One of the nice things about life in the lanes is its numerous peddlers, each with his particular call or identifying sound. The scissors grinder strikes on metal, the ice cream seller claps on wood, and the rag picker rings a bell. The tofu seller unfortunately has gone high tech and uses a loud speaker.

Lane dwellings are the preferred housing of the more enthusiastic Shanghailanders, especially the younger set who are willing to give up a certain amount of convenience for the privilege of living there. The housing ranges from the shabby to the stunning, with the latter much in demand and the prices reflecting this. For the more modest and somewhat renovated dwellings the prices can be quite reasonable — by Shanghai standards anyway — meaning between US$2,000-3,000 per month.

(5) Luxury apartment blocks. There are many top-of-the-line apartment buildings in the city, erected by foreign or joint-venture companies. They meet the foreigners' expectations and are usually filled with foreigners. They feature fitness centers, sports facilities, in-house shops and services, everything you have back in your own country. The waiting lists that formerly plagued these choice buildings have now evaporated due to increased competition, although the prices have held firm at the top of the range. (It will be interesting to see if, after so many years in a seller's market, these too are now forced to come down a bit.)

(6) Standard apartment dwellings. New apartment blocks are springing up like weeds (and are just as attractive), to the point where there is now a real glut in the market and one can be extremely selective. You pay for what you get so scout around and be sure that the bargain you are getting is really a bargain. Litigation between tenants and landlords is beginning to emerge as one of the offshoots of "misunderstandings" (if not downright misrepresentation). The facilities and services may be somewhat sketchy and the workmanship not all that you desire, as these buildings are being thrown up with alarming speed and shortcuts, but the range of choices is enormous. If you can find an expat tenant in the building of your choice to talk to privately you may be able to get the real dope on what the building's problems are; otherwise you will simply have to guess — and hope for the best.

(7) Living with or among the Chinese. This is not really an option if you are seeking a "legal" residence (more on this later) but it is done and it is the cheapest way to go. Here you are truly Mixing with the Masses (see MMM, Chapter 2) and this may be an option you wish to exercise only later, after you have perfected your Chinese language capability and have gotten a feel for what is involved in living a semi-Chinese lifestyle. As with many things Chinese this route is not for the faint of heart and a certain amount of hardihood is required.

Now that you know your options how do you find these places? If money is no object and/or your employer is footing the bill then your problems are merely those of choosing among many offerings. Here you will want to use one of the ubiquitous real estate agents to make your job easier and to give you the most options.

In the recent past, however, it has suddenly become possible to Do It Yourself. You can walk into the lobby of any apartment complex you spot that appeals and simply ask the management what is available and at what price. There will usually be a great deal and the prices are suddenly very negotiable. (We are told by reliable sources that the current vacancy rate for foreigners' dwellings built within the past twelve months is a mind-boggling 85%!) There are possibly perils in dealing without an agent to protect you (assuming that he or she is protecting you and not the owner) so *caveat emptor.*

If you do go the D.I.Y. route the *Shanghai Star* newspaper (see the following chapter) has a weekly column of real estate ads and there are often For Rent notices placed on the bulletin boards of the supermarkets frequented by foreigners. In your or your spouse's office there may well be Chinese employees who have decided to rent out premises they own, some of which they have done up to Western standards with an eye to that market, so you might want to ask around.

Once you get your housing problems solved then you must take care of obtaining the "Big Three": Residence permit, work permit (if you are employed) and multiple entry visa. We assume your or your spouse's office is taking care of your work permit; they are supposed to in any event. In most cases they will also assist you in getting your residence permit but this will call for more active participation by you. This may include several trips to the Foreigners' Entry and Exit Permits Division of the Public Security Bureau (PSB), currently located in their brand new building at 333 Wusong Lu in Hongkou District north of the Bund. (We also hear of foreigners who have been working here for ages by simply renewing their tourist visas but this route does require some tricky maneuvering and should be used only as a last resort.)

Among the items you will be asked to produce to obtain a residence permit at this critical office is a rental contract showing that you are residing in a "legal" residence, i.e., one that the owner has registered with the Shanghai government and in which foreigners are allowed to live. Unfortunately, if the owner registers his property as one for rental to foreigners he has to pay a whopping 21% tax on the income earned therefrom. Needless to say not too many owners are eager to register their properties and thus you have some perfectly lovely dwellings that may be "illegal," i.e., either unregistered or foreigners not permitted to live there.

If you rent one this can present some problems that you will have to overcome. We know people living all over the city in "illegal" dwellings so there must be ways to do it. Once again you will simply have to ask around. Try to ask the right questions of your prospective landlord at the very beginning, however, and this may avoid a lot of *mafan* (aggravation, trouble) later on.

Another piece of paper that you will be asked to present in order to obtain your residence permit is a government-certified (chopped) certificate of good health, which must include test results proving that you are HIV-free. Even if you have gotten a thorough examination in your native country and even if you have a paper attesting to that with all the chops and seals and whistles and bells that your government can provide, that cuts no ice here. You will have to either be re-examined or else have your previous examination "certified" by the Chinese medical staff at (are you ready?) the Shanghai International Travel Health Care Center which is located in Shanghai's western suburbs at 1701 Hami Lu.

One of our expat friends had warned us that this was a mind-boggling process and that rather than go through it again she would rather not work in China. Facing that delightful prospect we went, fearing The Worst — and had a grand time! First of all you must be the first one in line as this is one of the few places in China where (to all appearances anyway) it is first-come-first-served.

Get there at 8:00 a.m. (You must allow for the fact that it's out in the boonies about half an hour taxi ride away from almost anywhere.) You might want to call first (6268-7606) and be sure they are indeed open the day you want to go; you never know and you don't want a long ride for nothing. The taxi will drop you at the gate. You walk to the back of the compound to the last building on the left (you can ask the gate guard for directions but he will only gesture vaguely in that direction anyway). Have a seat; we suggest the one nearest the office door, remembering those horizontal queues.

By the way, no matter where you go in China unless you are loaded with inner resources you will always want to carry a book. You will be surprised at how many novels you can go through just sitting around waiting for things to happen. While others are fretting and fidgeting you are back in Tara or Manderly and you couldn't care less until it all gets worked out. (We even read in taxis; it saves us from flinching at the impending accidents unfolding all around us.)

Wait serenely and you will eventually be welcomed into the inner sanctum by someone in a white coat, possibly a doctor (who knows?). Present your medical examination papers if you have them or be prepared to take a complete physical examination right then and there. Your author's papers were up to snuff and, perhaps because she did not appear to be in a high-risk category for AIDS, it all went swimmingly.

This might have been due to her habit of always chatting up everyone in sight. She found that the doctor she drew was planning to attend a medical conference in Miami Beach, one of her favorite Tropical Deco destinations, and they were off. By the time she left, much of the lapsed time having been spent chatting rather than getting down to the business at hand, she had given the doctor lots of tips on what to see and had in return gotten her certificate, suitably chopped. All this was done with dispatch, courtesy and a modest fee, all after some rather pro-forma and non-invasive medical tests. Your experience may not be so benign but it will surely be interesting anyway. And since it is also necessary you may as well just make the best of it.

There are still other requirements for the residence permit, all of which are posted (in Chinese, of course) on the reception room wall at the PSB. If you do not speak Chinese it is imperative that someone from your office — or at least a Chinese speaker who can crack the code — go with you to help you wind your way through the labyrinth.

In dealing with the PSB your office must in any event be involved, as they will need to provide lots of the paperwork: the company's certification, the original (a copy won't do) of your work contract and your health certification plus your work permit, your passport, some completed and signed forms and probably other papers we never thought of. We really can't imagine your being able to work it out alone and if you can you certainly don't need to be reading this book.

And don't dawdle; the fine is RMB 500 a day if you exceed the number of days permitted between your arrival and the assembling of all the required documents (shoot for a maximum of two weeks). All this will probably take several trips to the PSB but eventually you should emerge with your three vital documents in hand: work permit, residence permit and multiple-entry visa. Without those it is hard to get anything done in Shanghai so give this chore your highest priority.

You've gotten your residence and now your residence permit so what other hurdles do you have to jump? The worst is over never fear and you may now concentrate on furnishing your new residence. You will find that almost everything you can possibly need can now be bought in Shanghai. Although the quality of China-manufactured products may not yet be quite up to Western standards it is improving steadily (and indeed many Western products are now being made here). At considerably more expense (to make up for the high import tariffs) there are also imported appliances available, the preferred ones being Japanese.

There are, for instance, "mega marts" of all sorts in Shanghai. These are gigantic Japanese, overseas Chinese, and foreign joint-venture stores. There is even the Chinese equivalent of the Price Club where you buy a membership for a modest amount of RMB and then can buy in bulk at considerably cheaper prices from its large warehouse-type store in the suburbs. (See "X" MARKS THE SPOT under *Shanghai, A to Z* at the rear of the book for listings of stores and sources.)

As mentioned in our Preface the Project HOPE publication entitled *Surviving in*

Shanghai tells you exactly where to buy almost anything you might want, down to the smallest nail. Since that book was completed, even more Western stores have opened. You can buy lovely export-quality material for draperies and slipcovers and have them professionally made, you can have furniture upholstered or even made to your specifications (if you have the time and patience) and you should have no problem in creating your own versions of Gracious Living with reasonable dispatch.

If you have children you will need to get them into school shortly after your arrival and we certainly hope you made inquiries before you came. The schools in Shanghai are getting more and more crowded and the costs, including the mandatory purchase of debentures in some cases, are spiraling.

Luckily you now have the choice of

several alternatives in the way schools, although they all come out at about the same cost. The Shanghai American School (SAS) is one of the oldest and uses the American curriculum. The new Shanghai International School (SIS) uses the British system, as does the Shanghai Singapore International School (SSIS) located on Sun Island near Suzhou. The Chang Ning International School shares a campus with the No. 3 Girls' School, one of Shanghai's best (it was formerly the prestigious McTyeire Girls' School, also the best in old Shanghai). There is also the Shanghai High School International Department and German, French and Japanese schools. (Again see "X" MARKS THE SPOT at the end of this book for addresses and telephone numbers.)

Your first step should be to contact the consulate general of your own country, most especially if you are interested in enrolling your child in a school with other children of your nationality. (You should also register there as a resident shortly after arriving.) It is also possible to get your children into Chinese schools, if they either speak adequate Chinese or are interested in learning it, but even the cost of these has escalated to the level of the international ones. (It is also possible that the educational credits from the Chinese schools may not be transferable to schools in the West upon your child's departure so check out this option carefully.)

If your child is still very young there are kindergartens and play schools as well as a play group organized by the Shanghai Expatriate Association (SEA). In some cases there are ones organized by residents of the apartment complexes most favored by foreigners. In any case your child will be well taken care of wherever he or she winds up; the Chinese adore children. Your main problem will be that Chinese ayis can never seem to say "No" to a foreign child, not an ideal rearing technique.

Have we solved all your settling-in problems yet?

We hope so and would like to point out in closing that Shanghai is becoming more sophisticated and more Westernized every day. The problems that many of us "urban pioneers" faced earlier are now just ancient history. The flow of information is more plentiful, we can now log onto both e-mail and the Internet, and we have easy access to four English-language publications (which we cover in the next chapter).

The range of Western facilities and services is fast approaching world class. You've come to Shanghai at the right time, at a time when, as the song goes, "the living is easy." Let's hope you grow to like this fabulous city at least half as much as we do.

Chapter 5

SO GET ON WITH IT ALREADY

We've outlined some of the problems you will have to face in integrating yourself into Shanghai life, or in creating a life of your own here, and we've insisted that you must make some choices along the way. Now we will present you with ten possibilities we think have merit — and might be fun to boot. There are probably many more out there that we haven't even thought of so don't let us limit your scope. Surprise us: come up with something new.

But first a little philosophical aside: To be really happy in life the experts (and anyone with common sense) will tell you that you must find something that seizes your interest and makes you long to know more about it, to do more with it, to pursue it avidly and make it your own. In our native countries this is easy; we grew up there, we speak the language, we know the customs, we know the options, we have the road map.

This is obviously more difficult in China (although mercifully less so in Shanghai we think) where both communications and Chinese customs challenge us and where the map is missing — or worse yet it's in Chinese. If you are ever going to be satisfied with your life here, however, you must find a role for yourself, either in the expatriate or Chinese community. Of course you can always be a mushroom and live in the dark but that is not an option we list for you here; we have far greater hopes for you.

The expatriate community is the easiest place to begin your quest. There about 40 nationalities represented in Shanghai, the SEA at present has 1300 members and the membership is still growing. More than half of them are wives. That leads us to category one:

A Tai-Tai

The term loosely translates as "lady," usually married and of the educated or upper classes in China. The term is often used somewhat derogatorily here in Shanghai to refer to idle wives who have nothing better to do than be chauffeured to shopping or to while away the hours lying on a chaise longue eating chocolate bonbons and reading bodice-rippers (the trade name for romantic trash novels). There is nothing wrong with being a Tai-Tai but the last thing we want you to be is idle, remember?

The typical Tai-Tai is most likely to be found in the more elegant restaurants, in the best hotels or their fitness centers, in the grip of expensive tailors or the fame-named boutiques that now abound in Shanghai (a city where the average local income still hovers around fifty U.S. dollars a month). Recreational shopping is the sport of the day and we don't knock that — in fact have written a section on it (see Category R at the rear of the book). The best thing is that there are always other Tai-Tais around to share the fun.

It's the Gilded Cage all over again but if that's what you like so be it. Not everyone is cut out to be Mother Teresa; it is perhaps sufficient that you occasionally feel a little twinge when you realize that the meal you have just eaten costs something like three months' salary of the waiter standing behind your chair. You may always ask, after all if no one eats those meals then the waiter has no job and is that any better? A valid point.

You are a lucky Tai-Tai to be in China. There are not so very many places left in the world where one can buy goods and services as cheaply as here (although prices are climbing at an alarming rate). Local manicurists, pedicurists and masseuses are still happy to come to your home and even the tailors make house calls. If you spread the word that you are interested the jade man, pearl man, linen man, Jin Shan (a local naïf painting style) man, paper-cut man, artists galore, all will be at your door in a trice. You need not even leave home to purchase goods or services — it will all come to you, as it did for Shanghai's Tai-Tai a hundred years ago. Some things do not change.

What is wrong with this picture? Nothing at all. We should all live so well. But one question does arise: Do I really need to be in China? Or perhaps more accurately, am I in China? That is for you to decide.

Let us now move out of our cloistered existence into category two:

An Explorer, or the Eternal Tourist

Everyone needs to be a bit of an explorer in China, at least initially; how else will you find out what everything is, where everything is, why everything is?

The first thing you do is buy an English-language Shanghai map; then you buy yet another Shanghai map, this one with Chinese characters. The latter will not only show you the bus routes but will be invaluable when you are in the hands of the usual clueless taxi driver, the Shanghainese who doesn't know where anything is in Shanghai and who cannot read English. Try to figure out in advance where you want to go so that you can at least point to the general location on the Chinese map. Although you may wind up having to do a bit of walking upon alighting at least you will be in the ballpark, so to speak.

Your third purchase should be some books starting with a good guide book. Our personal preference is the Odyssey guide book series (and not just because your author has two articles in it). The one on Shanghai gives you really good, comprehensive cultural and historical background information on the city and is also lively to read. Whatever your choice be sure the guide book covers not only the city itself but also the area surrounding Shanghai; there's lots of good stuff no more than 25 miles from the Bund that you will want to visit.

For an in-depth look into Shanghai's history we recommend *A Short History of*

Shanghai by Dr. F.L. Hawks Pott, the former President of Shanghai's most prestigious university, St. Johns. He wrote it over fifty years ago but it's a classic work that covers Shanghai in its hey-day. There is a reprint currently available in Shanghai's major hotel book stores. For a more lively history, that of Shanghai in the 1920's and '30's, you should seek out the book by Lynn Pan (Pan Ling is her Chinese name) called *In Search of Old Shanghai*. Luckily a new edition has just come out and is also available in Shanghai's book stores. These two books will get you started on the road to discovery in the most delightful way possible and they are both exceedingly good reads.

Although the state-run book stores, called "New China" or "Xin Hua Shu Dian," have most of the big-name books you may do better at the book stores in the major hotels. The old Jin Jiang Hotel has an excellent one beside the south gate, the Peace Hotel and the Nikko Hotel have them in the lobbies and others have them stashed away somewhere on the premises. You may pay a little more for the books there (note how they discreetly cover up the list prices with their own stickers) but it saves you a lot of hassle when you are new in town and green as grass. Later you can and must browse at Xin Hua's to keep current; but by then you will know the language, right?

Your fourth purchase should be either a serviceable pair of walking shoes or a bicycle — at least if you are anywhere near the age and body type where the latter would be appropriate. (Your author has been told that Chinese ladies over fifty never ride bicycles, or perhaps no Chinese ladies ride bicycles, what do we know?) We can assure you that the howls of horror that you will get from your family, your friends and most especially the Chinese will make it well worth the effort. You will be killed, you will be maimed, you will fall off, you will crash or be crashed upon. Yes, possibly, and that's before you even start pedaling.

All of this can of course also befall you while strolling on a local sidewalk (remember Chapter 2). If the idea of pedal pushing terrifies you then forget it — but you will have missed the absolute best way to see the local sights on pleasant sunny days or possibly, as a sop to the scared, only on weekends when there is theoretically less traffic on the roads. Downtown Shanghai has been so gerrymandered that it is impossible to know which streets even allow bikes these days so we are thinking more in terms of the residential districts and the suburbs. The city center you can reserve for your bus rides. And should you think that only bike riding can brings screams of horror just wait until you state that you are going to ride local busses.

But first, about those bikes. Do not, repeat not, buy a costly and conspicuous model unless you have very good locks (and more than one per bike please) and safe storage facilities. Stealing bikes is Big Business here. Despite increasing prosperity there are still plenty of people around Shanghai who cannot afford to buy a bike. Your author knows; she has already lost four or five (she also lost count). If you only paid fifty bucks for one the loss will not be too painful. The only problem with a local bike is finding your particular Flying Pigeon among all the other Pigeons parked around you.

Some insist that your fifth purchase should be a good accident insurance policy. Our rejoinder is that we all have to die sometime. Console yourself with the thought that anything that befalls you here will certainly make for a more interesting obituary than dying in bed back home. Moreover no matter what alarmists say, by staying in the middle of the pack, getting off and walking the bike when you feel intimidated, and concentrating only on what is going on in front of you and not what disasters lurk behind you, you'll probably have no problem. (Hey, this is China — we make no guarantees.) In passing please note that your author is a Little Old Lady, bikes all over the place, is not only still alive but has never broken anything — which should prove something. (Maybe she has biking karma?)

In this book we hesitate to recommend any items or services by name as they invariably disappear just after you have recommended them. We are going to take a chance, however, and state that your very first tour of Shanghai should be on the bright red Jin Jiang Tour Bus which leaves from the side door of the Garden Hotel on Mao Ming Nan Lu just opposite the Jin Jiang Hotel. It runs about every half hour and you purchase your ticket aboard. The price is currently RMB 18 but it will surely rise; Shanghai is the land of creeping prices.

The bus takes you to Ren Min Square and stops in front of the new Shanghai

Museum; the Orient Pearl TV Tower in Pudong; the Yao Han Department Store (also called "Next Age" and by the Chinese "Ba Bao Ban"), Shanghai's biggest bargain store and Pudong's drawing card; back across the Nanpu Bridge and to its base, where you can ride the elevator up and walk partway across it; the Old City Temple area in Old Town; Ren Min Square again, giving you another shot at the Museum (for which you should allow at least several hours); and then back to its starting point.

The nice thing about the Jin Jiang Tour Bus is that you can get off at any stop and then reboard a later bus (save your tickets); they even give you a schedule. Unfortunately it is in Chinese but by consulting the back of your ticket where the stops are written in English you can figure it out. So convenient is this bus that many Chinese families now use it to make shopping trips to Pudong; it's cheaper than a taxi over and back. You can still get a seat, however, and it is an excellent way to orient yourself in the first weeks of your Shanghai sojourn.

Now on to the busses that are not tour busses (those were the easy ones). If you don't read Chinese (who does? — save one billion Chinese of course) lay your two maps side by side and write the bus route numbers on the English-language one. Circle the location of your home and see what lines are near it and where they go. Shanghai is blanketed by bus and subway lines and the stops show all busses which stop there. Although there may sometimes be quite a hike between stops, with a little advance planning you should wind up near where you want to go. Most of the time.

If bussing is beneath you (elitism is allowed) do keep in mind those rainy days or rush hours when taxis are simply not stopping and you need to be someplace *now*. More than once your author has hopped onto a bus and made it, when taxis failed her, because she happened to know which bus went where. (Would you believe she found a neighborhood bus that goes right to the front door of the Concert Hall? She hasn't missed an overture since.)

Consider the case of Chinese New Year (or Spring Festival, as the authorities prefer to call it). Your author had a house guest. They dined out and found afterward that about fifty people in their locale were fruitlessly hailing the one or two available taxis still on the streets. After half an hour it became obvious that they were never going to get a taxi. Never mind. They nipped down to the nearest bus stop and along came a bus headed right to their home neighborhood. (Of course your author knew this because she had been studying her map.)

The good news is that they got onto the bus (with generous use of elbows) and homeward they went. The bad news is that at every stop another mob of failed taxi-hailers also got on. When the bus reached their stop and the front door opened another twenty were fighting their way onto it and there was no way they were going to get off. Wedged at the front of the bus, practically on the driver's lap, they could only throw themselves on his mercy.

Like the gallant gentleman that he was (and a dumbfounded one at that — he had never had a foreigner on his bus before) the driver opened his side door, leapt out of his seat and gently lifted his two fragile lady passengers out the door and onto the curb far below. Smiling cheerfully he got back into his bus and drove off. Would this happen in New York City do you think?

If you have the intestinal fortitude for busses then ask a Chinese friend or your ayi to go out and buy a pad of fifty tickets at five mao each (RMB .50), the basic bus fare. Then you just peel off one (or two for long rides) and drop them in the fare box in the new-fangled busses or hand them to the conductor in the old-style ones. Incidentally if you can tell her (there are seldom men conductors) where you want to get off or better yet, show her your destination in writing, you can rest assured that not only she but all the passengers in your vicinity will make it a point see that you don't miss your stop. (Bus riding is a chore and they welcome anything to liven it up.)

The Chinese are friendly to foreigners, except for the occasional grump you come across, and want you to like their country. They can be especially kind and helpful to older folks. Of course they can't help you when there are 200 passengers on a 100-passenger bus so don't expect miracles. If a super-crowded bus comes along just wait for the next one — they come about every five minutes on the main routes. (Your author will admit to occasionally giving up and hailing a taxi.)

We must in all fairness note that our house guest, the fellow bus-rider of the narrative above, assured the author that her expat readers would hate her for even suggesting such folly as the public bus. We admit it's an acquired taste but after all we did get home that night — and with a "Shanghai Experience" thrown in. If you are convinced that you will hate it then just keep this option in your hip pocket as an alternative when all else fails. (You'll thank us for this some day.)

One word of warning for future bus-riders, not of the dangers of the road but of the pocket. Pick-pockets abound on local busses (and elsewhere too for that matter) and even the conductor will warn you — not that you would probably understand her. She will possibly even keep an eye on you. But of course you must really learn to take care of yourself in the Big City. (We once had a house guest pickpocketed within hours of arriving in Shanghai — and he was from New York City!)

The Chinese have a saying that roughly translates as: he who allows himself to be stolen from deserves to be stolen from. So be sure to keep your money separated into Big Money and Chicken Feed and when using small change don't flash the larger bills about. There are currently in China no bills larger than a hundred but you don't want to flash a hog-choker roll of them about either.

Of course you must keep your passport near to your heart where it belongs, and a photocopy of the picture page at home so that replacement is easier if you do have the misfortune to lose it. If this does happen, however, do not panic; most Consulates General have a duty officer on call 24 hours a day for these and other such emergencies.

Now that we have made an explorer out of you what are you going to explore? Every single thing of interest in Shanghai of course. For starters do your homework and decide what is most interesting to you personally. Then have a Chinese friend write down a few key words of the area you wish to visit, maybe some street names, a temple name, something to hand someone if you get lost — as you inevitably will. Grab a guide book, a map, a notebook, a camera, a friend and a taxi.

No, no, we never said you could never take taxis. We only urged that you not take them exclusively and for your entire Shanghai stay. If you are new in town and have not yet figured out where everything is then of course you must rely on taxis (God help you) or a chauffeured car if you are that fortunate. The latter will, however, really cramp your style by keeping you tethered to it — to say nothing of driving up

the prices of everything in its vicinity when you alight.

But don't rely on taxi drivers to get you anywhere; that's the advantages of the busses — at least you can see the route they will be traveling and there probably won't be a surprise for you at the end of the journey. The surprise being that you are not anywhere near where you want to be. That's why you need the destination written out in Chinese; it's no guarantee but it will help. By the way, always carry your own home address in Chinese on you; we've known newcomers who couldn't get back home. It happens.

The nice thing about Shanghai is that if you go far enough in any direction you either hit water (north, east, south) or the airport (west). By the way, don't let the taxi driver take you over any bridges or through any tunnels unless you happen to want to visit Pudong — which you eventually will but not when you are aiming for the Bund.

A bit more on taxis (will it never end?). Luckily for us the fare fiddling that occurs in many neighboring countries, where they don't put the meter's flag down when the journey starts, is not a problem here (so far). The meter even registers zero for the first twenty meters so that if you change your mind and leap out the driver is not stuck with making good what is on the meter when there is no passenger to pay it. Why should you leap out? The local wisdom says that if a taxi driver does not know where the Portman, pronounced Poh-ta-mun, Hotel is, get out — he's hopeless.

Because of traffic congestion the Shanghai government keeps changing the rules. Currently odd-numbered taxis can go into the city center only on odd-numbered days and even-numbered ones on Tuesdays, Thursdays and Saturdays, so don't take it personally when the taxi driver you hail somehow conveys to you that he can do you no good. He risks a big fine and Big Trouble if he goes down certain central streets after 9:00 a.m. If you are only traveling around the suburbs then you have no problem but check the license plate's last digit if you wish to go to "downtown" Shanghai.

By the way did you know that the smaller taxis are somewhat cheaper at flag fall than the big luxury models (we use the term loosely here)? In any case when arranging your daily stash be sure you have lots of tens and fives; Shanghai taxi drivers too are part of the worldwide breed that never has change. We don't want you taking cabs exclusively but we certainly don't want you acting like a duffer when you do. Now aren't those prepaid bus tickets looking better all the time?

Well, if you're going to be an explorer, you may as well also be:

A Photographer

Looking back over the pictures we have taken in Shanghai for the past sixteen years we find that the ones that we most enjoy are the street scenes. Even in that short span many of the activities, and even the clothing, we captured on film are no longer seen on Shanghai streets. Pictures of China's monuments abound in magazines and books but the little details of everyday life are more elusive and — to us anyway — infinitely more interesting.

It is for you to decide what you want to capture, what you want to remember about Shanghai. Or if you are truly talented, what pictures of Shanghai would best sell, would be easiest to place in magazines. The photographs in this book are by the professional Shanghainese free-lance photographer Erh Dongqiang (AKA Deke Erh, the co-author of our five volumes), who has photographed in all of China's thirty provinces. What he has not captured on film he has collected and brought back to his folk art museum in the countryside outside Shanghai. He has never run out of subject matter nor interest in the things around him.

Professional quality film is available in a few camera shops in Shanghai, albeit at a somewhat higher price than in Hong Kong or the USA, so that need not be an excuse not to photograph. In her modest endeavors the author uses the current equivalent of a Brownie box camera and imported film that costs only RMB 20 per roll and is available everywhere — and the results are not all that bad.

Where but in Shanghai on a hot July day can you catch a cricket seller with his hundreds of tiny wicker baskets, each containing a cricket, affixed to a fishing pole he carries along? Or a lady washing her cat in a spittoon? Or any of the thousands of outdoor activities that take place in the lanes and alleys of Old Town, especially when the heat drives the inhabitants from their tiny homes? Go up in a tall building and photograph the rooftops beneath you; there is a whole world up there that we bottom-dwellers never see. (We find that some of the best gardens in town are up there on the rooftops.)

Our specialty is Western architecture. We never dreamed when we started photographing it in Shanghai those many years ago that ours would be the last record of many of the fine old buildings now sledgehammered into oblivion. Maybe yours will be the last record of other aspects of old Shanghai that are rapidly disappearing. Even if you don't do a book think how delighted your great great grandchildren will be to come across a dusty trunk containing a treasure trove of photographs of old Shanghai as it existed back in the bygone nineties.

It is of course not always as easy to photograph people and we have no special

techniques to recommend. Common courtesy requires that you ask the subject's permission (if you are spotted that is); if it is refused then that's that. It would obviously be foolish for you to try to photograph something that puts your host country in a bad light (any more than you would want that done in your own country) but within reasonable limits and with discretion there is no reason why most activities you choose to photograph should cause you any problems. If they do just cease and remove yourself from the scene; since you live here you can always come back another day.

Children are the most delightful subjects and Chinese children most especially so with their sparkling black eyes and beribboned pigtails. Their parents (or more often grandparents) are always happy to share their child with your camera. The problem may well be keeping all the other parents with children away once they spot what you are doing. This is especially the case if you are shooting with a Polaroid camera; that is an almost automatic invitation for a mob scene. Sometimes the parents will write out their address and then you can send them a copy of the photo. (Just paste what they wrote on an envelope and mail it; it usually gets through.)

In photographing almost anything except children we do trust that you are not one of those people who makes a big production out of snapping a picture. If you have to take time to set up, if you have a lot of elaborate and expensive equipment and if you make a fuss about it all, then unless you are under official sponsorship and have permission you are asking for trouble. But if you are a simple tourist or resident taking shots for your own album and if you move quickly and quietly (our only recommendation) then all of Shanghai is there for the taking. After all what's the point in seeing all the great things out here if you can't bore your friends back home with them later?

Well, if you're going to do all that exploring and photographing, you may as well go on and be:

A Historian or a Writer

Of course you don't have to be both but one logically leads to the other (or so we have found). You can keep it simple; start out with a diary or a journal of what you have seen and done. Again, remember those great great grandchildren. And remember also that the backbone of the sociological and historical knowledge that we have today was provided by those who, in all ages since the beginning of recorded history, wrote down everything, from the simple things that made up their daily lives to the great events that played out around them. Who knows — you may turn out to be the Samuel Pepys of Shanghai.

We've urged that you go see every single thing the guide books suggest. But what's the good of seeing it all if you have no idea what it's all about, how it fits into the Big Picture? If you are lazy then you just read what snippets of history the guide book's authors have selected for you —that's what they pay them those big bucks for — but if you are of a scholarly inclination then you would want to pick out something of especial interest to you and research it a bit deeper. Wouldn't you?

Nobody needs to know everything about everything, historically speaking, but as a minimum you should know about the Great Wall, the Grand Canal, who the last Dowager Empress was and how did she get there (and more importantly stay there for fifty years) and a bit about those terra-cotta warriors in Xi An — you know, all the fun stuff. OK, who can remember all those monosyllabic names of Emperors? (But cheer up, China only has a hundred surnames.)

Perhaps you would rather concentrate on Shanghai's more recent and much racier history. Luckily, you can actually visit the homes of most of the star players. There's Dr. Sun Yat-sen's home (the Chinese call him Sun Zhongshan) at 7 Xiangshan Lu and that of his wife Song Qingling (at 1843 Huai Hai Zhong Lu) who outlived him by nearly half a century; and the many homes of her sister Song Meiling, better known as Mme. Chiang Kai-shek, and her husband the Generalissimo, both in Shanghai and at Moganshan and Lushan, the local summer resorts. There is the home of Zhou Enlai at 73 Sinan Lu; and Chairman Mao Zedong stayed in many homes as did his wife Jiang Qing who was a local girl. (For a more complete listing see "Top Twenty Tourist Spots" in *Shanghai, A to Z*, at the rear of the book.)

Yuan Shikai once lived here, before he became China's would-be emperor. (Alas, he failed in that bid and died before realizing his dream of restarting the dynasty.) The most famous of China's 20th-century writers, Lu Xun, lived on Shanyin Lu, just south of Hongkou park, and his house is now a museum of his work. It is also a museum of the times, offering a rare opportunity to see the inside of one of the old lane houses and how life was lived in them. Then there was Du Yuesheng, boss of the infamous Green Gang and the most powerful man in all of Shanghai, more powerful even than any contemporary Mafia boss in the West could hope to be.

Shanghai also did not lack for Western luminaries of more honorable achievements: General George Marshall lived here for five years (we describe his mansion later in this book), and Lindbergh and Einstein both visited, as did Mary Pickford and Douglas Fairbanks. It was in Shanghai that Will Rogers opined, "We've got enough wrong with our own country without trying to tell the Chinese what's wrong with China." Wallis Warfield Simpson, before she became the Duchess of Windsor, lived here with her naval officer husband although nobody is sure quite where; it seems the Duchess kept the Shanghai portion of her past deliberately murky.

Count Galleazzo Ciano also lived here (he was married to Mussolini's daughter) as did Margot Fonteyn when she was a little Miss Margaret Hookham who loved to dance and starred in recitals in the Lyceum Theatre (which still stands). The greatest of the Russian ballerinas, Anna Pavlova, also visited, as did the Jewish musicians Mischa Elman and Ephraim Zimbalist. W. Somerset Maugham wrote here and Noel Coward composed, both while staying at the Cathay Hotel (now the Peace Hotel where the management will show you their rooms upon request). And do you remember World War II's famous U.S. Marine division that fought the Japanese so bravely on Wake Island? The survivors wound up in a P.O.W. camp just north of Shanghai, where most survived the war.

See what a little historical research opens up for you? There are probably loads of others who were here but who don't immediately come to mind. (We did this off the top of our head.) So it's not all just the same old boring stuff. So wouldn't you love to be the one to find out where the Duchess lived and what she really did here? (There are some pretty lurid stories about her Shanghai sojourn.) If Shanghai brought out the creative juices in Maugham and Coward why not in you?

There are plenty of research resources for the serious scholar in Shanghai but it may take some skill in getting access. In the artistic world you have the brand new and world-class Shanghai Museum on the site of the former race track. An equally stunning Municipal Library has just opened on Huai Hai Zhong Lu. In the western suburbs there are the Shanghai Archives and not far away the Shanghai Local History Museum. Every university has its own library and the ones that were formerly administered by foreigners, such as the Germans' Tongji University and the American St. John's, have volumes in several Western languages.

Best of all for the writer/researcher is the amount of free time made available thanks to the plentiful supply of full-time, reliable and affordable domestic help. Use wisely this boon, this gift of masses of time. You may never have it so good again.

We know everyone is not interested in research and writing (which leaves the field wide open for those of us who are, thank you very much). If this is not your thing, then why not go in the other direction and become:

A Student

Whether you wish to become a student or perhaps even better, a teacher, you've come to the right place. At last count there were 45 institutions of higher education in Shanghai. Not all of them need teachers and not all have open admission policies for foreign students but the range is certainly broad enough to give you some room for inquiries. We know that the top three, Fudan, Jiaotong and Tongji Universities, accept foreign students. For your convenience we have arbitrarily chosen the most likely 20 out of 45 institutions and listed them along with their addresses at the back of this book (see Category E in *Shanghai, A to Z*). There should be something there for everyone.

The very first thing you will wish to study, however, is Mandarin Chinese or if you are already fluent in that then perhaps the Shanghai dialect, which is a separate language unto itself. You are aware we trust that all the dialects spoken by the Han Chinese, be they Cantonese or Fujianese or Shanghainese or whatever, share a common pictographic form. Therefore if you learn to read and write the language you can always draw the characters in the palm of your hand when you are talking to someone of a differing dialect — a very handy technique.

If you like many of us are congenitally unable to comprehend the written language then just concentrate on speaking and understanding as much as you can. This alone takes a lot of hard work but it will pay off down the line as it will make your stay in Shanghai so much easier and more interesting.

We suggest you start off with a group class, preferably a small one (and don't worry it will get smaller with each passing lesson, trust us). This is not only an easy way to get to know other newcomers but it will also relieve you to know that you are not the only one who has trouble with the Chinese language. The friendships you form in these classes may well be the closest and most enduring; shared suffering tends to bring people closer together.

After you have graduated from the beginners' class then you will want to hire a private tutor. They abound in Shanghai so just ask around. The trick is to find one who is compatible with both your personality and with your learning style and needs. Therefore be sure to state firmly at the very beginning of a tutoring session that it is on a "trial" basis for the first month or so. That way if you turn out not to be soulmates and you wish to release that tutor and try another one you do not make him or her lose Face. You can always say you are going on vacation or that you have decided not to study Chinese after all. The tutor may know it's not true but it gives him or her a graceful out.

Some people have visual memories and some have aural and of course some have neither. You will have to find out what works best for you and then insist that the tutor use that method. If he can't or won't then get yourself another tutor. (Never fear there are hundreds out there.) A word of advice: Don't let yourself get bogged down in the minutiae; if you can't do tones then concentrate on words and move on.

It goes without saying that you treat your tutor as a colleague or guest and as such always offer a cup of tea or coffee at each visit. Regardless of age he or she should be addressed with the last name and the suffix "Laoshi" (pronounced to rhyme with "cows' fur"), such as "Wang Laoshi." Remember, this is an educated person who speaks your language plus Chinese — which is more than you do.

About that. After you gain a little fluency with the language you may wish to change tutors and go for one who speaks only Chinese. That way you will be able to resist the temptation to chat away in English (which the tutors are always eager to improve) and will have to concentrate on the subject at hand, learning to speak the Chinese language.

So what will all this cost you? Considerably less than language instructions in your own country. Inflation is rampant in Shanghai so you can no longer pick up a competent tutor for a dollar or two an hour, but it should not go much over RMB 100 an hour, depending of course on whether you have hired a PhD from a major Shanghai university or somebody's kid brother or sister fresh out of high school (in which case you can dispense with the Laoshi honorific).

The key is compatibility. With luck you will bond with your teacher. After all you have a common basis in struggling toward a common goal. In passing it is worth noting here that the relationships you form with your tutor, your ayi, your hairdresser, your tailor — all the significant people who interact with you to help make your life easier — are as important in your Shanghai sojourn as those with your friends, indeed some would say more so. If you care about and for them they will indeed probably become your friends.

Now that we have your Chinese studies under control let us move on to a yet more lofty plain. Shanghai's various universities, along with some commercial ventures, offer courses in everything from evaluating porcelain to seminars on China's broad history and culture. These are usually announced well in advance in one of four publications, all of which you will want to seek out and subscribe to.

Twice weekly there is the local English language newspaper called the *Shanghai Star*. There's a page called "What's On" that tells you what's on (what else?) in Shanghai. *Culture and Recreation*, a biweekly publication, overlaps a bit but there is always something new. Then there's the monthly publication *Shanghai Talk* which covers events in more depth and also has a "What's on" column. Finally the Shanghai Expatriate Association's monthly *Courier* covers even greater ground as they also announce their own bountiful events (most of which are not listed anywhere else). You must of course be a SEA member to receive their newsletter but you would want to become one in any event; it should be your first order of priority in the socializing segment of your settling-in process.

With these four publications you can keep abreast of cultural, recreational and educational offerings,

indeed a generous range of them. If you choose to fill in gaps in your cultural upbringing and not just with Things Chinese there are many visiting European and American dance and theatre troupes and even more musical ones. (See the later section "Music Maven" for more detailed information.)

The cost of these activities will be minimal and the returns enormous. If you decide not to avail yourselves of these opportunities so be it — but we don't want to catch you complaining that there is nothing to do in Shanghai.

Not of the scholarly persuasion? Then try the other end of the spectrum and become:

A Teacher

If you have full accreditation and a teaching certificate from your home country then there may be openings in the multi-national schools for substitute teachers, depending of course on your specialization and your flexibility. The number of international schools in Shanghai is growing yearly. There are currently ones offering curricula in the English, German, French and Japanese languages, with schools of other nationalities slated to come.

If your qualifications are not so documented and yet you want to do some teaching, almost all the local private schools are looking for native-speaking teachers of English and in some cases of other European languages. The pay will not be much but the rewards will be tremendous. Western teachers here in China are universally delighted (and often overwhelmed) by the dedication of their students and their eagerness to learn, often to the exhaustion of the teacher. Accustomed to more lackadaisical performances in their own countries they find the thirst for knowledge of the Chinese students a refreshing change.

How to get these teaching jobs? You ask around. For instance your author's interest in music led her to tutor some musicians in her spare time. If your interest is cooking or the service industry then check with the hotels which cater to foreigners. (Just call the manager, who is usually either Swiss or German). If you have a specialty that employs a technical language then seek out others of that ilk in technical schools. The employees of your office or that of your spouse can be helpful in this regard, just as they will be for many other questions and requests you have (our "ask around"). If that's not part of their job at least in most cases they are too polite to say so. (And they may well wind up asking you to tutor them.)

If you do not wish to tutor languages your options are more limited. The Shanghai Expatriate Association holds classes for expats in all sorts of things, all done on a volunteer basis and a great way to meet members of like interests. For instance, in previous issues of the SEA newsletter under the heading of "Small Groups" the following were listed: Aerobics, Arts and Crafts, Bible Study, Book Club, Bowling, Bridge, Choir, Flower Arranging, Mahjong, Mothers and Toddlers, "Music in a Band," Photography, Quilting, Silk Painting, Tennis, Conversational Spanish and Conversational Chinese. There was also an Internet users group, a self support group, and groups organized by nationality.

In case none of this appeals, their closing sentence should: "Ideas for new small groups are always welcome." Perhaps you can be the first in Shanghai to teach some new and esoteric hobby or sport. You are sure to find kindred souls among a membership of over a thousand expatriates.

As for the Chinese as soon as the word spreads that you have a specialty in which they are interested they will seek you out; in fact, the Shanghainese' desire to learn new things from the West is so great that you will probably be swamped. Remember,

there are thirteen million people in Shanghai and its environs. To give you only one example, a small notice appeared in a local newspaper stating that a neighborhood "Children's Palace" was offering Saturday morning English classes for children. Can you guess how many children showed up to register? Three thousand. Need we say more?

Enough of philanthropy or low-to-no-paying jobs, you say. If you are a person of experience and business acumen then you may wish to consider becoming:

A Businessperson

If you spot openings here for someone of your unique talent then go for it. That is what draws the Westerners to invest in China in droves: the knowledge that there is a one-billion-strong market here for something, if they can only figure out what it is that the Chinese need or want and can afford (the last is the tricky part).

Starting with opium and real estate (and we recommend neither) fortunes have been made here in Shanghai and can be again. If you do not wish to concentrate on the Chinese market then consider the large expatriate one, some product or service that Shanghai's foreigners need and that you or your company can best provide. The path to setting up a company in China is not an easy one and we can't tell you how to do it but expats somehow do it all the time without our help.

There is abundant help to be gotten through publications of the Chambers of Commerce of the various nations represented in Shanghai, which now has 31 consulates general (up from five when your author arrived in 1981). The Chambers also hold discussions and seminars on various business-related topics and meet informally to share and solve problems. In addition there are professional courses taught by various enterprising business mavens. (See what we mean about finding something the foreigners need?)

Every time we go into a book store in the United States or in Hong Kong we are struck by the number of new "How-To" guides focusing on China: How to Do Business in China, How to Invest in China, How to Negotiate with the Chinese and on and on. Like the self-help and self-improvement book market in general this little niche is growing exponentially and with good reason. The "consultancy" business is also growing apace and for the same reason: doing business in China is tough and you'll need all the help you can get. So avail yourselves of all the free and for-pay professional advice available. Then when you succeed you can do a role reversal.

By the way, if you are here on a spouse's residence permit you will need to find out what sort of business activities you are or are not permitted to do. Or perhaps not.

Some schools of thought maintain that it is better never to ask anything here, lest you be given a negative answer (which you probably will). We can't advise you on that, and we never promised you a rose garden, but if business is born in the blood then you will somehow figure out how to proceed.

In our "Success Stories" chapter we even tell you of some who succeeded, but obviously not of those who failed. (There are no "Failures" chapters in up-beat books like this.) Oh yes, and we do wish you luck. You'll need it.

If you are not motivated to set up your own business then there are possibilities of working for expatriate companies already set up. Due to a recent change in the rules, obtaining a work permit is a bit harder than it used to be, or so we are told. But it can still be done and once again

"*guanxi*" is helpful here. As it is in life in general.

Foreign companies are hungry for good help, especially if the help already has a residence permit (and can be called a "local hire" so the company doesn't have to provide housing) and if the help also speaks Chinese. OK, one out of two's not bad. Ask around or "network" at Chambers of Commerce, the Expatriate Professional Women's Club, or other expatriate meetings. You should also inquire of your own consulate general; some hire their countries' citizens for non-sensitive work that they cannot find a Chinese or a consular spouse to perform.

Cannot find or don't want a paying job? Then be:

A Philanthropist

No you don't have to have masses of money to give away. We mean philanthropy in the pure sense of the word: give of your time and your talent. For all its progress China is still a poor country, especially once you get away from the glittering thoroughfares of Shanghai and provinces of the "gold coast" that surround it. Shanghai has homes for the aged, for retired nuns, for the infirm, for orphans, for the handicapped, centers for the reemployment training of laid-off workers, and other social services, hospices, etc. This is a newly emerging phenomenon in China and these groups can all use help.

You don't have to be a trail-blazer; in most cases others have gone before you. For instance the Shanghai Expatriate Association has done a tremendous amount of charity work in almost all the categories listed above. They hold fund-raising events to buy equipment and, better yet, they do hands-on work: they go to the needy organizations and volunteer services as well as money.

The orphanages immediately come to mind, possibly because they have gotten so much bad publicity lately. Some expat families wind up adopting baby girls (there are few baby boys for adoption in China for reasons you can surmise). If you love children and yours are far from you, then you can cuddle and play with these abandoned tykes and give them the love and attention that the local under-paid personnel in the understaffed facilities simply can't or won't.

Natural disasters periodically ravage China so there are clothing drives for flood victims, food collections for the needy and charity donations of a personal kind, as opposed to the massive ones where you are not quite sure just where the money winds up.

A group of expats recently set up "Operation Sunrise," a hands-on foundation which helps students from the poorest of the poor families (earning below RMB 250 a month) stay in school. Here you sponsor a child, whom you meet and get to know personally. You interact with the family and get to watch your money actually benefit the child. Can you think of any better way to give to a charity or cause?

China's needs are great and the Chinese are trying to meet them but with their enormous population and concomitant housing squeeze the government's task is almost overwhelming. This is most especially the case in cities like Shanghai, where millions of migrants flock to the city seeking work. China needs all sorts of help, if you can just figure out how to give it; no country (and especially China) wants to admit it needs help from foreigners. Once again, turn to those who have already forged the links.

We have not dealt with religion and the role of the churches in China (nor will we) but there are thousands of active churches and the congregations outgrow them daily. If you are a practicing Christian or of the Jewish faith then go to church (there are no synagogues presently open in China) or seek out co-religionists and find what charities they support. For Catholics there are Sunday morning masses in English and Latin. For Protestants there is the former Community Church, just opposite the old Shanghai American School building, which not only welcomes foreigners but also provides special seating and simultaneous translation devices for its Chinese services every Sunday morning. Recently a non-denominational Protestant fellowship group of expatriates was given permission also to meet there later in the day.

These congregations will be able to direct you toward a number of worthy causes, some church-related and some not, and can supply you the information you need to make further choices. If your time is limited then perhaps giving money will suffice but it is the giving of your time and your efforts that makes philanthropy truly rewarding. There is certainly a place for that in China.

If you are musically inclined or trained perhaps you would rather give of your talent and become:

A Music Maven

A recent arrival lamented that there was so little in the way of musical offerings in Shanghai, a statement that stunned the author, who attends live concerts at least once a week here. Shanghai has a rich and varied musical life, on a par with that of any major city in the world. It has one of China's two music conservatories, with its Sunday night concerts costing twenty-five cents (US) per ticket and featuring China's (tomorrow the world's) best young talent. The auditorium is a bit of a barn (wear warm clothing in winter) but it is acoustically adequate and the range of talent in it is superb.

We have watched miniature virtuosos of ten (who looked to be about six), whose feet could not reach the piano pedals — which had to be extended with blocks of wood — play like angels. One year the Conservatory had a Christmas pageant with just that: choirs of Chinese angels carrying lighted candles and proceeding down the center aisle, all singing "O Come All

Ye Faithful" in English. This in the heart of Communist China? It was a moving Christmas eve event.

There is a local (Western) opera company whose recent production of Turandot was outstandingly sung, to say nothing of a Peking and a Shaoxing Opera Company (in the latter all the major roles are sung by women). The singers often perform in concert, sometimes selecting scenes from a popular Western opera with four or more singers in full regalia singing its duets, trios and quartets — and in French or Italian to boot.

If you have not sat through a Peking or Shaoxing Opera, we might add, you have not truly experienced China. You must not be put off by the likes of P.J. O'Rourke, who describes Chinese opera music "as if a truck full of wind chimes collided with a stack of empty oil drums during a birdcall contest" — even if that is an accurate description.

The most fun is observing the audience's behavior that we suspect has changed little over the centuries, except that hot towels are no longer flung to recipients over the heads of the crowd and the sweets hawkers wait until intermission to shout out their wares. The audience is both vocal and mobile. They chat at full conversational level throughout, sometimes about the plot but just as often (as nearly as we can determine) about domestic problems and the world situation in general. This does not seem to faze the performers, who soldier on while people get up and leave or arrive an hour or two late (which brings us only to the first intermission) or wander

around volubly greeting old friends. Most of the activity in the theatre, in fact, is not to be found on the stage.

Children race up and down the aisles, sometimes loudly calling for parents they have lost. Everyone eats constantly, a particular favorite being sunflower seeds whose hulls are spat indiscriminately in all directions. The lyrics are projected onto the wall just beside the stage and people often help their neighbors by reading the text aloud. Everyone seems to know the plot (except for us foreigners) and the only hush that ever descends on the auditorium is when a "superstar" is due to appear (usually quite late in the performance) or a particularly intricate or treacherous business is about to occur. The audience then sits up, shuts up, watches that bit, applauds and then goes on about its regular business.

They all have a jolly good time and you will too — at least once. Admittedly Chinese opera is an acquired taste. But like the Ring Cycle it is something that everyone should sit through once; it will teach you discipline and endurance if nothing else. We've read of rare foreigners who gets intrigued enough to study Chinese opera (see the section on "Going Native") and who have even passed auditions to enroll in Peking Opera Schools in China. (By the way, this is an option we hadn't thought of.)

We have never heard of any Westerners subsequently being hired by a Chinese opera company, as it takes many years of training to reach the required level of artistic proficiency in both its specialized and highly nasal singing and its stylized movements. Presumably these Western students go back to their native countries and dazzle them there.

Let us turn from this esoteric realm to the Western music with which we are more familiar. There are two symphony orchestras in Shanghai, the Shanghai Symphony Orchestra (SSO) being the better one and the Shanghai Broadcasting Symphony Orchestra the richer (from all that radio revenue). The SSO has successfully toured in Europe and the Americas. Here in Shanghai it often hosts performances by guest conductors and soloists from the West.

Because the Chinese government subsidizes the orchestras only to the extent that it pays the musicians' salaries (and there are over a hundred musicians on each orchestra payroll) the orchestras must seek funds from other sources to support themselves. In the case of the SSO it not only seeks sponsors from the business community but also hires out its rehearsal building as a dance hall and disco when it is not being used for practice sessions. The SSO performs in the Shanghai Concert Hall, a lovely old auditorium in the classic style that, surprisingly, was once a cinema called the Nanking

Theatre. (We have a great photo from the 1930's of a ten-foot tall plywood Tarzan swinging from its elaborate marquee.)

If you are a talented musician the orchestras might be interested (with sponsorship help) in having you perform with them. If you are, like most of us, only a music buff then there are ample opportunities to become a part of the music community through a combination of philanthropy (see our previous category) and volunteer work (see our Teacher category). With a generous donation of money and time you might even be appointed to their Board of Directors.

At the very least, if your genuine love of music shines through, you can get to know personally some of these fine performers and perhaps become a part of their musical community. (You can also hire them to perform at your own soirees, which really adds a bit of class to the social events.)

The easiest entree into the music world is through attending the last — and our favorite — of the listing of musical events: the Friday night Chamber Music Concert Series. This one has been going on for years and just moved to an ornate salon on the ground floor of the Jing An Guest House, where there is a performance every Friday evening at 8:00 p.m. No reservations are necessary and the tickets cost RMB 20 at the door. (Where could you ever find such a deal in the West?)

Because the same music lovers attend Friday after Friday, year after year, they all get to know each other, they grow to recognize the musicians and if they spot a particular talent they can always make inquiries and perhaps find ways to help that student. (China's students often come from poor families.) This is philanthropy that pays you back in spades; you not only sponsor young talent but you get the pleasure of listening to them perform and improve, knowing that you played a small part in their improvement. That's why we listed this particular category next to the Philanthropist one; it is our favorite and most rewarding charity.

We've only hit the high spots here so let's not hear any more nonsense about there being no musical offerings in Shanghai. There are many ways to become a member of Shanghai's music community, by philanthropy, performing, organizing a chorus or choir of expatriate singers, or loaning your own personal music scores to a group to copy (they could use some Boccherini; he doesn't often get played because the scores are not available in Shanghai). There is a sea of talent to listen to and enjoy or to support in some way through your good offices. Your own musical world will be richer for the effort.

We are now at Category Ten and the last one that you can be, indeed that most of you will, no matter what your efforts at integration, always be:

A "Laowai"

This term basically means "old foreigner" and is not necessarily pejorative — although it can be, depending on the tone with which it is uttered. Unless you are of Asian origin you can not escape your face in China: you are a *da bizi*, or "big-nosed" foreigner and that is that. You will always stand out in a crowd — although in recent years it is no longer possible to attract a circle of twenty or so by just standing there breathing as was the case in the early 1980's.

We have always maintained that China is a great place to be if you are an egomaniac or if you thrive on attention. You will always be the center of it here. You will never pass down a street unnoticed (most especially by beggars near the major hotels) or do anything that does not elicit interest on the part of some Chinese, be they mere passers-by or professional guides paid to look after you (once called "barbarian handlers" here). The sophisticated Shanghainese can almost always identify your nationality by the cut of your clothes, the shoes you wear, the language you speak or the accent of the Chinese you speak. There is no hiding place.

If you are an Asian unless you make a real effort you will still stand out, will still be the outsider. For starters our Asian friends tell us that they are treated much less politely than are we Westerners. If you are of Chinese origin then after one look at your face the Shanghainese will expect you to speak Chinese. If you do not then you have an additional handicap; at least they don't expect that of us Westerners. Only if you are ex-Shanghainese and not too far removed will you be able to really reintegrate yourself into local life, albeit never again completely we suspect.

We need not give you a lecture here on not letting the team down and all that sort of thing. You must always keep in the back of your mind, however, the fact that anything you do, be it good or evil, will surely be expanded to cover all others of your nationality. (This is not uniquely Chinese; we Westerners too have that mind set.) Flashes of frothing anger, unmitigated rudeness or condescension, all the negative stuff that may merely be a facet of your own complex personality — or of just having a bad day — will not rest solely on your shoulders. It will be stored away somewhere by the onlooker and subsequently applied to all others of your nationality. It doesn't seem fair, does it?

The flip side is that the Chinese are forgiving. Good will and good acts can often cancel out bad ones. So shouldn't we make it a point as often as possible to do some good and thus stockpile for all the bad stuff that will surely come down the pike? Common Courtesy, the Golden Rule, the Ten Commandments, the whole schmier, is a great deal better than the opposite, at least to the recipient.

Never fear, we don't expect you to be eternally, supernaturally and uninterruptedly a paragon of all the virtues. (Even your author, who prides herself in her saint-like disposition, has been known to froth and flail about on occasion.) Living in China as in any foreign country can be trying to say the least. On some days your frustration level will be such that you may pride yourself in having enough self-control not to do bodily harm. Just keep saying to yourself, it's their country, I am only a guest. If you think you have problems just imagine what the Chinese have. All you need to do is try to get along, survive, and return to your own country — where you can then do things your way. The Chinese don't have that option.

The bottom line is: Wouldn't you rather have your Shanghai stay be one of getting to know China and its customs, one of challenges met and challenges overcome? Wouldn't you rather be renowned here, in legend and in song, as that wonderful American, or British or German or Italian or whatever, teacher or philanthropist or perhaps merely friend who once dwelled in this city and then went away — but who left a mark, made a difference and is not forgotten? (Perhaps that is a form of immortality; anyway it's what keeps us slaving away here.)

Your contribution may be tangible — a book, a scholarship, a child still in school, a charity enriched, an orphan with a better life. Or it may be only in the memory of man. You have the choice of how to interact and what to be. You can fritter away your stay, forget it and be forgotten, or you can do positive things for yourself and for the Chinese people and enrich all your lives.

The U.S. Army has a recruiting poster which admonishes: Be All That You Can Be. The choices are here. It's all up to you.

Chapter 6

SUCCESS STORIES — THIS COULD BE YOU

As we promised you previously here are some success stories — the names omitted to protect the innocent — of people who came to Shanghai, found their niche and lived happily here. (The failures you will have to ferret out on your own.) In several cases this was a first overseas tour, some of the people involved were by no means sophisticated world travelers, and many had no gift for or interest in foreign languages. Yet even with these handicaps they could and did find happiness and fulfillment in Shanghai and in some cases helped other foreigners do the same. In many cases they were also able to make a difference in the lives of the local Chinese.

Let's start with a man, in this case not a spouse but an employee of an American firm. His job is challenging but he does not have the companionship of his wife, who has a job in the USA and comes out only once or twice a year. Since he has chosen to forego Shanghai's hotspots, karaoke bars and nightclubs, you might think Mr. A's evenings boring, right? Wrong.

This gentleman, strong of wind and limb (and getting stronger every day), has chosen to walk. And we mean walk. He gets up early every morning and utilizes every weekend walking — up to 20 miles (35 KM) a day. He also walks nights after work. He has walked almost every neighborhood, every road, every path, every village, every hamlet, everywhere within a 25-mile radius of Shanghai. He probably knows more about Shanghai and its environs than any foreigner here. In fact if we needed to

learn of Shanghai's problems, to know what is really going on here, we would turn first to him.

Can you imagine what he observes on his daily walks? He knows which areas are blooming and which are failing, which enterprises are prospering and which are moribund. He knows what's been torn down and when and what's going up. He knows the crops, the farming techniques, the changes in the countryside, the fast-changing of weather fronts. He knows anything anyone could possibly want to know about the real Shanghai, the Bund and beyond — well beyond.

Mr. A knows a little Chinese, has a cheerful demeanor and an inquiring mind, gets along well with all sorts of people and, we are sure, will be one of those foreigners who go down in legend, perhaps as The Stranger Who Walked (and Walked and Walked) Among Us. We envy him his fortitude and his stamina — to say nothing of his vast storehouse of Shanghai knowledge.

Mrs. B is a housewife who loves children. She and her businessman husband live a privileged life in Shanghai but their children are grown and flown. She volunteers several days a week at a local orphanage, playing with abandoned babies. Her successes? Children who could neither walk nor talk because of lack of stimulation now can do both. Just imagine the joy of watching a small child come to life in your hands. These babies will never know who or what saved them. Mrs. B knows. She made a difference.

Mrs. C was one of those human dynamos who was into everything here. The spouse of a busy executive, she and a few other wives started up a small group of bored housewives — originally 35 — which they named the Shanghai Expatriates' Association. The Association now numbers over 1300 members and is still growing. She helped organize their "small group" activities (taught bridge, took silk painting) and ran all of their tours, first in Shanghai and later all over China.

She searched out Chinese groups needing help, the retired nuns, the old folks, the orphans, and got the small expat community into action to collect and buy the items that these people so badly needed. She helped the SEA deliver them personally and she periodically checked back to see if they were being used by the intended recipients.

Mrs. C then started a play-reading group of young Chinese girls to help them improve their English, encouraged them to study abroad and provided the loans that were needed to do so. To this day those girls, who mostly work abroad as successful middle managers, keep up with each other and with her. Her house in the USA is still a way-station for Chinese visitors, whom she continues to advise and motivate (and if anyone could get you moving it would be she).

Mrs. C has a commanding personality and does not take "No" (in China it's actually "no way" or "meiyou banfa") for an answer. At a time when foreigners were scarce and facilities few she created activities and opportunities and laid the groundwork for one of the most effective hands-on charity operations in Shanghai, one that continues today. This lady made a difference.

Mrs. D is a born businesswoman but with a busy executive husband it took her a while to find her role in Shanghai. Initially she helped launch the career of a promising young artist. Then she launched her own career as a relocation specialist, then her own company. So busy and successful was it that she brought over her children to help her manage it.

She is an elegant and forceful lady who won as her clients some of America's top corporations who were starting up businesses in Shanghai. We understand her venture was a financial success from the very first, a rare phenomenon in a city where the start-up cost for companies is high. She not only has a thriving business here but is now also able to be with her children and grandchildren. We asked her how long she plans to stay in Shanghai. Her answer: "Indefinitely."

Mrs. E, Mrs. F and Mrs. G are the wives of diplomats stationed in Shanghai. All are Asians; two are artists and one is a well-known calligrapher. Here they are able to study under the tutelage of famous local masters, to mount exhibitions and to sell their works. They are an integral part of the art world and are sought after for gallery and exhibition openings and for advice to local artists on the art world of the West. They are helping others all the while they are improving their own artistic techniques. Where else could they find such a fortuitous confluence of artistic talent and training possibilities? Shanghai is a happy posting for them all and their works reflect this.

Mrs. H is a mezzo soprano, the wife of an executive. Here she too could get excellent coaching, give concerts backed up by the Shanghai Symphony Orchestra and sing leading roles in operas, both here and in neighboring countries. She was also able to help and to inspire local vocalists and to broaden their musical horizons through the loan of music scores. She has now returned to her own country where she still pursues her musical interests. Her stay in Shanghai was another step in her musical career.

Mrs. I is a born cook. She utilized her Shanghai stay to study and refine her Chinese cooking skills. She then passed these on to others by starting a round-robin cuisine club that met and cooked in the members' homes around Shanghai (much to the delight of the spouses). She was instrumental in the preparation of an international cook book now sold here, with the proceeds going to charity.

Miss J was in the diplomatic service and had lived all over the world, so Shanghai was no special challenge, especially since she had adequate Mandarin Chinese upon arrival. Long a student of history and of architecture she combined the two by researching Shanghai's old Western buildings. When she realized that there were no books in English on this subject she joined up with a Chinese photographer and they began to produce them. At last report they had completed five volumes on western architecture in old China, all of which received international acclaim. All this was done in her limited free time, after work and on weekends.

Miss J is now a full-time researcher and writer for an international company and a research resource for the many visitors and scholars who come to Shanghai to learn more about the city. If it had not been for the concerted effort of this writer-photographer team there would be no visual or written record remaining of the thousands of old Western buildings that have disappeared from China's cities. By focusing only on one aspect of a wide range of possibilities, this duo was thus able to preserve one small segment of China for future historians.

Consul General K is the grandson of one of Shanghai's great Western taipans and also a historian and writer. While fulfilling all his responsibilities to a busy Consulate General he nonetheless managed to find time to complete the research on a book about his grandfather's business and life in Shanghai. While Ambassador in Beijing he got it published in Chinese and his next project is to get it translated into English. This will further increase the book's value to the world of researchers. Through his research he has gained insights into China that are invaluable in his diplomatic endeavors.

Mr. L is not only a correspondent for a major newspaper but he is also a renaissance man, a talented musician, a born researcher, a man who will get the most out of any country to which he is assigned. In Shanghai he has done just that. He is deeply involved in the musical world, where he helps struggling musicians get their act together — in the literal sense of the word. He shares his expertise and even his sheet music with them and encourages and fosters their careers.

A gifted writer, he also assists and edits other writers' work (including the author's) and promotes them in Shanghai and wherever and whenever he can. He does this, and many other services, for his foreign and Chinese friends alike, and is a constant source of encouragement and information for them. He loves Shanghai and gives it his all — and the city reciprocates. His life is busy, rich and varied. He is really making the most of his stay here.

We could go on and on but we think you get the idea. Find your niche in Shanghai and go from there. Bon voyage!

Chapter 7

WHITHER SHANGHAI, WHITHER YOU?

A long-departed friend who loved Shanghai wrote: "China slips slowly into distant memories. The bad times disappear and only the good times remain. We have given talks about our sojourn there but requests are fewer and fewer. We do still talk about it, but it has passed into our history..."

Shanghai will too one day pass into your history — and you are fortunate to be here in one of the most exciting times in its history. No place in the world is growing as fast as China. With the recent death of its patriarch Deng Xiaoping it is entering a new era of younger leadership. Its prospects — as well as its problems — are mind-boggling. No one can ever be sure how it will all turn out.

Living in China is not easy. In some ways it is a first world country, in some ways a third world one, both coexisting uneasily side by side. We have not gone into the many problems you may face here and you may subsequently accuse us of having emphasized the positive and glossed over the negative. That we cannot deny. We advocate the mind set of Churchill, who once admonished his wartime staff to present him only the positive aspects of the issue; the negative ones would soon enough make themselves apparent.

We foreigners are strangers in a strange land, often lost and frequently confused. But every day Shanghai will seem a little less foreign to you —or it should if you're doing your homework like we told you to. We have found that after most Shanghailanders have been here a while they develop a real affection for their host city. (We admit our study is skewed. We never get to ask the ones who hated it, as they have long ago packed up and gone home.)

There is a Jewish toast, "May you live in interesting times." In China and most especially in Shanghai we are fortunate to be present at the most interesting stage of its development and to be sharing in some small way in it. We are in the right place at the right time; many of us would not want to be any place else.

We only hope that you too can find something in the city that will make your stay worthwhile, that you will get something of value from the Chinese people and that you will be able to give something to them in return. That has been the focus of this book. Put your mind — and your heart — into this city and its people and they will repay you a hundred fold. This we truly believe.

A N N E X

SHANGHAI, A TO Z

ARCHITECTURE IN SHANGHAI

In 1981 when your author first arrived in Shanghai, it looked like a city frozen in time — that time being 1937, the year the Japanese came to Shanghai in full force. The city also looked like a cross between old Warsaw and contemporary Calcutta. In the area stretching westward from the Bund (an Anglo-Indian word meaning waterfront embankment) into the former French and international settlements you had a city of mostly Western architecture with a Chinese population crammed into it. The city was planned for about four million people — now there are thirteen million and counting.

The large amount of Western architecture in Shanghai is even more remarkable when you consider that at no time did the Westerners comprise more than five percent of the population. (For a breakdown of the foreign population by years, see the YESTERYEAR entry at the back of this book.) It was the Westerners, however, who controlled the city, and they built primarily to their own taste, when they were not building for quick profit the high-density dwellings for the Chinese population. (It is noteworthy that the basis of many of the fortunes amassed by the foreigners was real estate speculation.)

Initially all the major *hongs* had their offices on or near the Bund and each tried to outdo the other in erecting the most imposing edifice, one reflecting the architecture of the country from which they came — and to which they would ultimately return. The Bund has miraculously survived, although many of the fine interiors have been ravaged by heedless renovations.

Much is changed but much of old Shanghai has survived and in stunning variety: By the Garden Bridge the low white building in the British colonial style, formerly the British Consulate; the banking houses of the Bund, and right off it a Tudor-style beamed cottage, formerly Calbeck's wine store; farther along on Fuzhou Lu the former American Club, in the American (Southern, with columns) colonial style, even its bricks imported from there; the sumptuous mansard-roofed villa in the French Concession where General George Marshall once lived (and before him a French nobleman); the Savoy Apartments with their stunning Art Deco detailing, right down the street from Post Pottier, the former French police station in the style of Marseilles; the Normandie, a wedge-shaped building that would be right at home in Paris, from whence the architect came. Every country and every style is represented somewhere in Shanghai, and one of its joys is searching out and finding today the remnants of its Western world of yesterday.

The old buildings may be somewhat shabby and certainly chockablock full but they are still here, little islands of style in an ever-encroaching sea of faceless and mostly tasteless new high-rises. Look in any direction from Avenue Joffre (now Huai Hai Lu) or Bubbling Well Road (now Nanjing Xi Lu) and acres of shattered buildings greet you. The rubble resembles that of World War II's bombing devastation. Unknowing visitors must wonder what war occurred here — and so recently.

If Shanghai's ubiquitous karaoke bars are, as often maintained, Japanese retaliation for their defeat in the last war, then smoked glass and tacky lavatorial tiling may be Hong Kong's and Taiwan's way of cocking a snoot at their Asian neighbor. Much of Avenue Joffre, which once featured elegant French boutiques and cafes, has been renovated with a vengeance by overseas-based Chinese entrepreneurs and decorators. Its facades now feature everything from faux Grecian warriors bearing porticoes to pink plastic checkerboards overlaid with red lettering. Only a few of the plane trees, planted by the French so long ago, have survived the recent road-widening.

The glory of the old hotels is, however, undimmed and several have been renovated to near their former splendor. The Peace (formerly Sir Victor Sassoon's magnificent Cathay Hotel) still leads the way, its renovations based on the original plans. Its distinctive black and red pinnacled roof is still a landmark on the Bund. It is interesting to note that the present lobby occupies only half of its previous area; even in China it is hard to dislodge sitting tenants.

The Park Hotel on Nanjing Lu opposite the old race course and the Cathay Mansions, now the Jin Jiang Hotel on Maoming Lu, evoke only a pallid version of their glorious past. Opposite the latter the old Cercle Sportif Francais has been incorporated into the Garden Hotel and beautifully restored by its Okura owners, even down to the sprung floor in the elliptical ballroom. And no matter what their current state no one could ever accuse these magnificent old hotels and clubs of becoming Plastic City.

Many of the old high-rise apartment houses still survive, mostly built in what was then the new and stunning Art Deco style. Many had descriptive names: the Cosmopolitan, the Uptown, West Gardens, Tiny Mansions, Cavendish Court (this one Tudor), the Gascogne, the Picardie, the Normandie (these three in Frenchtown, of course). In the suburbs old housing complexes such as Granada Estates and Holly Heath are still there, dwarfed now by towering monoliths of concrete and steel. Our first book on Shanghai's Western architecture, A LAST LOOK, contains a listing of nearly three hundred apartment houses starting with the Aida in Frenchtown and ending with the Yuen Ming apartments near the Bund.

For the moneyed classes, the taipans or top echelon of Shanghai's business hierarchy,

there were magnificent estates with large gardens (now mostly full of miscellaneous and ugly buildings). They ranged in style from a Gothic fantasy to a mock-Tudor country estate, the former belonging to a Swedish shipping magnate, the latter to Sir Victor Sassoon, who also had a private golf course adjoining (now the Shanghai Zoo). Between these extremes were numerous mansions in the French, Spanish and English styles, homes of expatriate barons and dukes, taipans, triad bosses and KMT high brass. Today the most magnificent ones are occupied by foreign consulates or offices.

These old Western buildings, and only these buildings, will preserve for Shanghai the atmosphere and the elegance that the new buildings can never equal. Perhaps in future years the symbol of Shanghai may be that of the lofty suspension bridges that span the Huangpu River, linking old Shanghai with the new Pudong Development Zone on its east bank. Or perhaps Pudong's new Orient Pearl TV Tower will become that symbol (although we fervently hope not).

At present, however, what represents Shanghai to most of the world is the Bund and the magnificent old structures which the foreigners built during their hey-day there. The eye is drawn again and again to their massive and stately beauty, stretching along the waterfront and down Nanjing Road. The foreign architects and tenants are long gone. They returned to their native countries, leaving behind them the edifices in which they had hoped to lay the foundation for future fortunes, for future empires — and which most occupied a scant two decades.

Shanghai's old architecture is testimony to a once mighty Western presence here. When that is gone — and it is going fast — the last remaining record of the foreigners' former presence here will be gone forever. Sic Transit Gloria Mundi.

...AND ALSO ASIAN

THE OLD CHINESE CITY (Nan Shi)

In the area of the Cheng Huang Miao (Temple of the City God) in the heart of Shanghai's Old Town there are scores of small shops that sell everything imaginable. One sells only corks and stoppers, another only buttons, another hair ornaments, another canes, another fans, and on and on. On the lane leading into the central area there is still the shop where Jiang Qing (Mme. Mao) used to buy her wigs and where you can buy one today. There are also shops selling *baozi* and *jiaozi* and *kebabs* and broad beans and many other local delicacies.

Right in the middle is the famous Willow Pattern Tea House and the Ming Dynasty Yu Garden, both reached by the Bridge of Nine Turnings — so constructed because evil spirits cannot turn corners. The Old Town is little changed. In its crowded streets you can truly mix with the masses and get the feel of what life must have been like for the Chinese in old days in Shanghai.

THE CONFUCIAN TEMPLE, WEN MIAO (on Wen Miao Lu in Old Town)

The Wen Temple, several blocks south of the Temple of the City God, has a little something for everyone: You-drive-it electric kiddy cars (like bumper cars, only smaller), electric boats, souvenir and snack stalls, TV games, a book market, a bird market which also has fish, hairy turtles and other pets, and of course its Confucian temple (*miao* means temple). For decades it has been a favorite of Shanghai children and it is filled with them on weekends.

It's a little tricky to find: Off Zhong Hua Lu, the ring road that encircles the Old Town, is Wen Miao lane. This circular road actually has two names: Ren Min Lu for the northern half and Zhong Hua Lu for the southern half; you must go around it clockwise, as it is one-way. The road was laid down on the site of the smelly creek and city walls that once encircled Old Town. Wen Miao is located near what was originally the old West Gate of the walled city.

A SHINTO SHRINE (on Zhapu Lu in Hongkou District)

To find this little-known but very interesting building go to Zhapu Lu, a north-south running street just north of Suzhou Creek. After you pass a large intersection with a cluster of three cinemas (once Shanghai's Broadway) and past a whole street of nothing but restaurants, then start looking to your left. There you will first see a lovely old house with a Japanese door frame of carved wood, then next to it a temple building. The roof is supported by an arch carved in the shape of a large lotus. There were originally carvings of elephants and other magnificent beasts above rows of chrysanthemums on its outer walls. The former were chipped away during the Cultural Revolution and only the chrysanthemums survive.

The building was used by the Japanese in World War II to store the ashes of their soldiers before they were shipped back to Japan. It is now a karaoke-coffee bar and nothing remains in the interior of its original splendor.

...AND IN THE ENVIRONS OF SHANGHAI

ZHOUZHUANG AND ZHUJIAJIAO (to the west of Shanghai)

Near Shanghai there are two Ming Dynasty villages which remain intact, Zhouzhuang and Zhujiajiao. The former is more difficult to reach. Zhujiajiao, is the first one you come to, just off the road leading westward to Shanghai's Dian Shan Lake. They both appear to be a towns that time forgot. The villages' stone bridges, picturesque lanes on the banks of its old canals and neighborhoods with old courtyards, all appear little changed over the centuries. (Like Williamsburg in the USA, however, this is deceptive; the Chinese government has spent millions of yuan on restoring the villages to their former state.)

Film-makers have now discovered Zhujiajiao and it was the setting of more than ten historical movies in 1996. Film-makers say this is because it is reminiscent of Shanghai in the 1930's and 1940's. To us it and Zhouzhuang are more reminiscent of villages of three hundred years earlier. They are charming places to visit, especially if you can arrange to be there when they are not overrun with hoards of sightseers like yourself!

Always with an eye to business the antique dealers have moved in among the villages' sellers of knickknacks and folk art but this is not bad news. Now in addition to seeing quaint villages you can also do a little shopping for exotic items that you cannot find in Shanghai (although most probably they were brought to the villages from there).

C KEEPING CRICKETS

"If a bird is kept for the sake of its song, why not keep a cricket for the sake of its chirp?"

There are references to crickets in the earliest Chinese literature but it was only in the Tang Dynasty (613-905 A.D.) that the Chinese began to keep them in cages. It was then that the care of crickets really developed into an art, but it was only in the Sung Dynasty (960-1280 A.D.) that the sport of cricket fighting started. The story of cricket culture in China, with its gourds, cages, clay pots, feeding pans, ivory and pigs hair ticklers, tweezers, traps, etc., is a very interesting one.

The fighting crickets (called *qu-qu*, as in Chattanooga Choo Choo) are captured toward the end of summer by dealers who scour the countryside for the best of the breed. Some counties are famous for having especially fierce fighting crickets and these traditionally command enormous prices even today when cricket fighting is outlawed. There are 67 varieties of fighting crickets and those that chirp the loudest are considered to be the boldest and fetch the highest prices.

In the olden days "young Chinese fanciers have been known to ruin themselves by investing in large studs of these insects, which are not only expensive to buy but also to keep. Very fine specimens are as expensive as racing ponies. They require special attendants, as horses require grooms, and separate stalls — earthenware pots lined with fine mold and fitted with a microscopic cup for their drinking water." These special clay pots are still manufactured today and antique ones are still available in the markets.

There were special diets for the fighting crickets, special medicines if they caught cold and even conjugal visits with "every male allowed to have a lady in his tiny earthen cage for two hours each evening." Before the big fight started the combatants were tickled with cricket ticklers. When they were released they flew at each other in a rage at having been so harassed. The winner bore the proud name of "Conquering Cricket" and upon his death was buried in a silver coffin "with the hope that more good fighting crickets, attracted by the honorable funeral, will be found next year near its grave." We have, alas, never found a silver cricket coffin in China.

What are still available, however, are the most wonderful of all the cricket containers, the cricket gourds. These are hollowed out, incised with designs or grown in molds which form them into weird and exotic shapes, often with the mold's designs pressed into them. The tops can be of ivory, jade, tortoise shell or simple bamboo, all carved with a design. The ones belonging to the emperors are truly exquisite and found only in museums but really fine examples can still bought (for high prices) in China's antique markets.

Also available and at more moderate prices are the contemporary cricket carriers for the smallest of the species, the *jinlingzi* and *huanglingzi* (loosely translated as

"golden bell singers"). Their homes are of plastic or wood and about the size of half a cigarette case. The plastic ones come in imaginative designs such as a TV set, a pistol or an automobile, and the wooden ones have lids, usually elaborately carved, which slide over their glass windows. All the cases have little plugs at the ends into which the food is inserted.

The most spectacular — and certainly most audible — of the many cricket varieties is the biggest of all, a gigantic green one called *jiao gu-gu* (rhymes with ow-oo-oo) in Shanghainese. These resemble gigantic grasshoppers. They are kept in cages and sold by itinerant vendors who carry hundreds of woven wicker ones on a fishing pole. They have no need to call out their wares as they pass by; you can hear them before you see them.

These crickets live out their days in cages, where they often hang upside down like lumpy hammocks. Their "song" (screech would be more accurate) is earsplitting and they are mostly relegated to outdoor locations. They are partial to green beans for some reason but also like melons and cucumbers, from which they get their liquid. It is not necessary to put water in any of the cricket containers as long as they get their veggies or steamed rice.

In the cricket season of late summer you can buy these and many other varieties in the local Bird, Fish and Flower Market. You can then place them all over your house (or out of doors in the case of the giant greens) so that you will have altos, sopranos, tenors, baritones, basses — a veritable chorus — singing away at you all day. Alas, they all live only a hundred days or so and when their short span is over you will find that you miss their cheerful chorus.

DIPLOMATIC MISSIONS

In 1930 Shanghai had eighteen Consulates General:

America	Austria	Belgium	Brazil
Czechoslovakia	Denmark	Finland	France
Germany	Great Britain	Italy	Japan
The Netherlands	Norway	Portugal	Spain
Sweden	Switzerland		

Shanghai now has thirty-one Consulates General, up from the five that were here seventeen years ago. For your handy reference we list them below.

Australia	17 Fuxing Xi Lu	6433-4604
Austria	Qi Hua Tower 3A, 1375 Huai Hai Zhong Lu	6474-0268
Belgium	127 Wuyi Lu	6437-7041
Brazil	Qi Hua Tower 10B, 1375 Huai Hai Zhong Lu	6437-0110
Canada	Suite 604 West Tower, 1376 Nanjing Xi Lu	6279-8400
Chile	Suite 3-5A, Equatorial, 65 Yan An Xi Lu	6249-8000
Cuba	55 Loushanguan Lu, New Town Mansion	6275-3078
Czech Republic	Qi Hua Tower 12B, 1375 Huai Hai Zhong Lu	6471-2420
Denmark	Suite 701, SITC, 2200 Yan An Xi Lu	6209-0500
Finland	Qi Hua Tower 7A, 1375 Huai Hai Zhong Lu	6474-0068
France	Qi Hua Tower 23B, 1375 Huai Hai Zhong Lu	6437-7414
Germany	151 Yong Fu Lu	6433-6951
Great Britain	Suite 301, 1376 Nanjing Xi Lu	6279-7650
India	Suite 1008, SITC, 2200 Yan An Xi Lu	6275-8885
Iran	Rm 1110, Jindu Bldg, 277 Wuxin Lu	6472-1389
Israel	Suite 703, 55 Loushanguan Lu	6209-8008
Italy	Qi Hua Tower 11AB, 1375 Huai Hai Zhong Lu	6471-6980
Japan	1517 Huai Hai Zhong Lu	6433-6639
Korea	4th fl., SITC, 2200 Yan An Xi Lu	6219-6417
Mexico	Qi Hua Tower 20B, 1375 Huai Hai Zhong Lu	6437-9585
Netherlands	4th fl. East, Sun Plaza, 88 Xian Xia Lu	6209-9076
New Zealand	Qi Hua Tower 15B, 1375 Huai Hai Zhong Lu	6471-1127
Norway	Qi Hua Tower 8A, 1375 Huai Hai Zhong Lu	6471-2986
Poland	618 Jianguo Xi Lu	6433-4735
Russia	20 Huangpu Lu	6324-2682
Singapore	400 Wulumuqi Zhong Lu	6437-0776
Sweden	Qi Hua Tower 6A, 1375 Huai Hai Zhong Lu	6474-1311
Switzerland	Rm 302 West, Sun Plaza, 88 Xian Xia Lu	6270-0519
Thailand	7 Zhongshan Dong Yi Lu	6343-4095
Turkey	Qi Hua Tower 13B, 1375 Huai Hai Zhong Lu	6471-2351
USA	1469 Huai Hai Zhong Lu	6433-6880

Because your author is an American we take the liberty of telling you a little bit extra about:

THE AMERICAN CONSULATE GENERAL

The present Consulate General opened in 1980, almost thirty years to the day from the time it last closed its doors in Shanghai. The earliest American Consulate was located north of Suzhou Creek in Hongkou in an area known as "Consular Row" where the consulates of Germany, Japan, Russia and the United States overlooked the Huangpu River. The British Consulate was nearby, just across the Garden Bridge on the Bund. Only the Russian Consulate General still occupies its original premises.

In 1930 the American Consulate moved into the Kalee Hotel at 248 Jiangxi Road at the corner of Jiujiang Road. From there it later moved to the Development Building on the southwest corner of Jiangxi Road and Fuzhou Road (across from the Hamilton House and the Metropole Hotel).

During World War II all the allied consulates closed, and the officers were put under house arrest until they could be exchanged for the enemies' diplomats. When the Communists arrived in Shanghai in 1949 the Americans started leaving and the consulates began drawing down. The American Consulate officially closed its doors on April 25, 1950.

EDUCATIONAL OPPORTUNITIES

In Chapter Five we discussed the opportunities for both studying and teaching and here we supply you with detailed information. If you are the mother or father of a student, or yourself a would-be student or teacher, then here is what you need to know:

INTERNATIONAL SCHOOLS

Shanghai American School (SAS)	TEL: 6252-1687
(Ronald Montgomery, Principal)	50 Jidi Lu, Zhudi Township
(three campus locations)	Minghang District (Main Campus)
Shanghai Chang Ning Int'l School	TEL: 6212-2328
	155 Jiangsu Lu
Shanghai International School (SIS)	TEL: 6242-3243
	11 Hongqiao Lu
International Pre-School:	
Song Qingling Kindergarten	TEL: 6242-9851
(Ages 3-6)	61 Hong Mei Bei Lu

Japanese School in Hongqiao
Shanghai Singapore International School (SSIS) in Qingpu, on Sun Island
French/German School
(For details on these schools, call the relevant Consulates General)

INSTITUTIONS OF HIGHER EDUCATION

East China Normal University	3663 Zhongshan Bei Lu
East China Science and Engineering University	130 Meiling Lu
Fudan University	220 Handan Lu
Jiaotong University	1954 Huashan Lu
Tongji University	1239 Siping Lu
Shanghai University	149 Yanchang Lu
Shanghai Normal University	10 Guilin Lu
Shanghai International Studies University (SIIS)	550 Dalian Xi Lu
The Textile College of China / CTU Lasalle	1882 Yan An Xi Lu
The Medical College (Medical School)	138 Yixueyuan Lu
The Second Medical College	200 Chongqing Nan Lu
The College of Chinese Medicine	530 Lingling Lu
The Industrial College of East China	516 Jungong Lu
The Ocean Shipping College	1550 Pudong Lu
The Music College/Conservatory of Music	209 Fenyang Lu
The Physical Training College	650 Qinyuanhuan Lu

The Drama College	630 Huashan Lu
The Finance and Economics College	777 Guoding Lu
The East China College of Politics and Law	1575 Wanhangdu Lu
The Shanghai Institute of Foreign Trade	620 Gubei Lu

In addition to these 20, there are 25 more colleges, institutes and universities teaching subjects ranging from Agronomy to Tourism. For a complete listing you may contact the U.S. Information Service (USIS) at Qi Hua Towers, 1375 Huai Hai Zhong Lu, 4th floor, TEL: 6471-8689 or your own national equivalent in Shanghai, the press and cultural affairs section of your Consulate General. (See "Diplomatic Missions" above for a complete list of Consulates General and telephone numbers.)

FINANCIAL MATTERS

Should the need arise there is no longer a problem of getting money fast in Shanghai. There are now ATM machines all over the city, which is good news if you have a foreign bank card. If you are on the Cirrus system there are two Citibank ATMs in the Peace Hotel on Nanjing Lu at the Bund. The instructions are in English and the machines will spit out a maximum of RMB 2000 per transaction — enough to get you through the day we hope. There is also an Emergency Cash ATM for American Express customers in the Shanghai Centre on the ground floor next to the Wellcome Supermarket. (The Amexco office is on the second floor.)

Hong Kong Bank ETC card holders can withdraw cash at the Industrial and Commercial Bank ATMs on the ground floor of the Orient Shopping Center at 8 Caoxi Bei Lu in Xujiahui. If you cannot crack the ATM code but are an Amexco, Visa or Mastercard holder you can cash personal checks at the Bank of China, either at the main branch at 23 Zhongshan Dong Yi Lu (next to the Peace Hotel on the Bund) or at their Nanjing Xi Lu branch next to the JC Mandarin Hotel.

If you are not holding the proper card, or when all else fails and you still need cash fast, don't despair; turn to your friendly Western Union. (It's great for having Mom wire money.) The local agent, the China Courier Service Corporation (CCSC), says they do cash-by-wire transactions in dollars or RMB. Money can be transferred to you in China from any of Western Union's 24,000 worldwide locations and it can be picked up at the CCSC office or delivered by courier. (The CCSC Hotline telephone number is 6356-8129.)

In Shanghai there are numerous branches of international banks but they are still hemmed in by various restrictions which we won't go into here, especially since they keep evolving. The best idea is to visit the bank of your choice and consult with the nice native-speaking customer representative there to determine if the bank can meet your financial needs in Shanghai.

To make it easy for you herewith are the names and addresses of some of Shanghai's major banking houses or banking representatives. New banks are opening daily (there are already over a hundred), so bear in mind that this list represents only a small selection of banks, chosen primarily for their convenient locations:

Australia & New Zealand Bank	Hotel Equatorial, 65 Yan An Xi Lu, 2-West
Bank of America	Union Bldg, 100 Yan An Dong Lu, Rm 1802
Banque Indosuez	Union Bldg, 100 Yan An Dong Lu, Rm 502-5
Banque Nationale de Paris	Jin Jiang Hotel, 59 Maoming Nan Lu, Rm 155
Bank of Tokyo	Ruijin Bldg, 205 Maoming Nan Lu, Rm 205
Barclays Bank	Shanghai Ctr, 1376 Nanjing Xi Lu, Rm 530-W
Bayerische Vereinsbank	SITC, 2200 Yan An Xi Lu, Rm. 1808
Chase Bank	Shanghai Ctr, 1376 Nanjing Xi Lu, Rm 700A
Citibank	Union Bldg, 100 Yan An Dong Lu, Rm 1904
Commerzbank AG	Central Place, 16 Henan Nan Lu, 7th floor

Credit Lyonnais	Central Place, 16 Henan Nan Lu, 6th floor
Credit Suisse	Shartex Plaza, 88 Zunyi Nan Lu. 11th floor
Deutsche Bank AG	Guangming Bldg, 2 Jin Ling Dong Lu,Rm 2501
Fuji Bank	Ruijin Bldg, 205 Maoming Nan Lu, Rm 1001
Hang Sen Bank	Ruijin Bldg, 205 Maoming Nan Lu, Rm. 1301
Hongkong & Shanghai Bank	185 Yuan Ming Yuan Lu
ING Bank	Central Place, 16 Henan Nan Lu, 2nd floor
Mitsubishi Bank	Ruijin Bldg, 205 Maoming Nan Lu, Rm 2404
Royal Bank of Canada	Union Bldg, 100 Yan An Dong Lu, Rm 403
Societe Generale	Universal Bldg, 172 Yuyuan Lu, 8th floor
Standard Chartered Bank	Shanghai Ctr, 1376 Nanjing Xi Lu, Level 7
Union Bank of Switzerland	Union Bldg, 100 Yan An Dong Lu, Rm 1904

Shanghai as a banking center is not a new phenomenon, merely a return (we hope) to its former role as the financial center of Asia:

---------- 1939 BANK LIST ----------

American Express Bank of Canton
- China
- Chosen
- Communications
- East Asia
- Taiwan
Banque Belge
Banque Franco Chinoise
Banque de l'Indo-Chine
Central Bank of China
Central Trust Co.
Chartered
Chekiang Industrial
China Banking Corp.
China Development Bank
China Expt., Impt., & Bank Co.
China Reconstruction Bank
China & South Sea Bank
China State Bank
Chinese Industrial
Chung Foo Union
Chung Hwa Comm'l.
Chung Wai
Chung Woo Com'l. & Savings Bank
Commercial
Continental
Cook & Son, Thos.
Deutsch- Asiatische
Discount Savings Bank
Foo Yuen Bank
Hongkong & Shanghai Bank

Italian Bank for China
Kiangsu
Kiangsu Farmers' Bank.
Kincheng
Kohan Trust
Land Bank of China
Manufacturers' Bank of China
Mercantile Bank of India
Mitsubishi
Mitsui
Moscow Narodny Bank
National City Bank of N.Y.
National Com'l
Nat. Industrial
Nederlandsch- Indische
Netherlands Trading
Oversea-Chinese
Ningpo Comm'l
Pootung Comm. & Savings Bank
Sassoon Banking Co.
Shanghai Bank
Shanghai Coal Merchants' Bank
Shanghai Commer.
Shanghai Mercantile
Sin-Hua Savings Bank
Sumitomo
Underwriters Savings Bank
Union Commercial Bank
Woman's Com'l, and Savings Bank
Yokohama Specie

GIFT GIVING AND RECEIVING ETIQUETTE IN CHINA

— *Gifts or other objects presented by one person to another are presented and received with both hands.*

— *Etiquette rules dictate that gifts must always be refused at least once, in order not to appear too eager.*

— *One should be careful not to be too effusive in admiration of objects or art in the home of a Chinese, as to the mind of the Chinese this savors of a hint that the guest would appreciate being presented with it.*

— *It is wise politely to refuse offers of presents unless one is convinced that there exists a genuine reason for their presentation.*

By Julean Arnold, the American Commercial Attache in Shanghai, 1926.

****

TIPS ON LUNAR NEW YEAR GIFT GIVING

You will need to give a "13th month" bonus to your ayis (pro-rated if they have been working less than a year for you) and of course a present would be nice. You can also spread other little presents around, depending on how helpful the doorman, guard, any service staff, have been to you (and what sort of service you wish to get from them next year). Little red envelopes (*hongbao*) with several small bills to the minor children of Chinese friends are always appreciated; they will be delighted that you know the custom.

For the Chinese the lunar new year is the equivalent of Christmas, New Year and birthdays all rolled into one. (Each Chinese is automatically one year older at the commencement of the lunar new year.) Your author has found that thoughtfulness and generosity are usually rewarded in many small ways over the year that follows.

By the author

HAPPY NEW YEAR — IN OLD CHINA

There are many small customs and superstitions connected with Chinese New Year. People's respect for supernatural powers and their desire to pacify them led to the creation of many taboos. These were to appease the gods or spirits, who were believed to be powerful enough to destroy everything in the world. Some of these customs are interesting and unusual such as:

— The first letter written on New Year's Day should begin with the characters for *wealth, happiness and long life.*

— Women must prepare everything ahead of New Year as the use of knives or scissors, both "lethal tools," is forbidden between the first and the fifth day.

— On the picture of the Kitchen God one should smear honey on its mouth so that he will have only good things to report about the family.

— In conversation no loss of money should be mentioned, one should not quarrel with nor scold a servant, nor chat directly after taking a bath.

— Children were especially warned not to use words of ill-omen, such as *demon, death, coffin, lion, tiger, elephant* and *snake.*

— Fearing that children might forget, parents might put up a strip of red paper saying: CHILDREN'S WORDS DO NOT COUNT.

— Changing dishes after one has started eating a meal meant death to the housewife.

— One should not lose one's temper or show any unhappiness or otherwise he or she will remain in a bad mood for the rest of the year.

— One must be careful not to stumble or fall when out calling, for that would bring bad luck to the home where the call was being made.

— One should not thread a needle on the 7th or 8th day after New Year.

— One should not start on a journey on the 7th, 17th or 27th, and should not return home on the 8th, 18th or 28th.

— The fifth day is known as "Break the Fifth" and on that day people are allowed to do whatever they like; that day marks the revival of routine life.

— One should start cleaning on the fifth day and all garbage, nicknamed "dirt poor," must be taken out. But one should never sweep the floor towards the door, otherwise wealth and good luck will be swept out of the house.

— If on New Year's Day the wind blows from the southeast the harvest will be good, and if it's cloudy food will be expensive.

All of this officially ended only with the Feast of the Lantern, on the fifteenth day of the first Chinese month. All taboos were believed to have lost their sacred power by then.

IGNORANCE OF CHINA

WHAT DO WE WESTERNERS KNOW ANYWAY?

"What does anybody here know of China? Even those Europeans who have been in the Empire are almost as ignorant of it as the rest of us. Everything is covered by a veil, through which a glimpse of what is within may occasionally be caught, a glimpse just sufficient to set the imagination at work and more likely to mislead than to inform."

> *Thomas Babington Mccaulay, British Secretary of State for War, in the House of Commons, April, 1840*

****

When you have been in China for one week,
you can write a book.

When you have been in China for one month,
you can write an article.

When you have been in China for six months,
you can write a letter to your friends.

When you are an Old China Hand, the best you can
manage is a short dinner speech,
reminiscing about your experiences...

****

The writer's authorship of this book calls to mind a poem written by the Chinese poet Bai Juyi nearly twelve hundred years ago:

> Those who speak know nothing;
> Those who know are silent.
>
> Those words, I am told,
> Were spoken by Laozi —
>
> If we are to believe that Laozi
> Was himself one who knew,
>
> How comes it that he wrote a book
> Of five thousand words?

JEWISH REFUGEES IN SHANGHAI

Shanghai as a refuge for Jews fleeing Hitler's Europe? Why would they come halfway around the world to a country whose language they did not speak, whose culture they did not share? They did come, however, about 18,000 of them, to live among the Chinese and to share their wartime hardships. Their story is yet another of the incredible stories of Shanghai.

These Jewish refugees came to Shanghai in three waves. First were those prescient Germans who saw the handwriting on the wall when Hitler came to power in 1933. Many were able to escape with both money and possessions, a luxury denied those coming later. The second to come were the Austrians, who left their country starting in 1938 when Germany annexed Austria to the German Reich, and the Germans, after the terrible pogroms in November of that year. A third and much smaller group of Polish Jews came shortly after Germany invaded Poland in September 1939.

All these Jewish refugees came to Shanghai because it was the only place in the world that would freely accept them; they had only to get here. There was initially no documentation, no formalities required to enter the city. It was accessible almost to the beginning of World War II by Italian steamship lines or by the more arduous overland route via train across Siberia to Japan and then by ship to Shanghai.

The refugees who arrived early were able to live and work in the French Concession and the International Settlement. Some were even able to start new lives in their old businesses and professions. All this ended in February 1943 when the Japanese, under pressure from the Germans, ordered all "stateless persons" to move north of Suzhou Creek to Hongkew (now Hongkou) District.

Their lives once again uprooted by relocation, the refugees were forced into a so-called "restricted area" — the words "Jew" and "ghetto" were never used — an area less than one mile square and already crowded with 100,000 Chinese. This was to be the final wartime home of Shanghai's Jewish refugees.

Hunger and disease were rampant, conditions were deplorable and as the war progressed they got worse. The refugees lived alongside the Chinese in the lanes, crowded into unsanitary tenement flats, often several families living together. They suffered great hardships but somehow learned to adapt to the spartan life of their Chinese neighbors, with whom they lived in harmony.

In this small enclave in the heart of a Chinese city, however, a distinctively Jewish cultural life began to emerge, a microcosm of the larger world that the refugees had left behind in Europe. The professionals, doctors, engineers, lawyers, professors, scientists, artists, singers, musicians, composers, conductors, stage stars, film directors, writers, poets, Yeshiva scholars and rabbis, all slowly began to rebuild their lives yet once again. The businessmen and entrepreneurs among them opened small business and service enterprises.

They attended services in the Ohel Moishe Synagogue, which still stands (now serving as a museum of the Jewish refugees and ghetto life in Hongkou). They published newspapers in four languages, held concerts, staged musical performances and cabaret acts, reconstituted the Yiddish theatre, established schools and training classes, held lectures, staffed their own hospitals and clinics. *Heime* (communal residences), organized with help from abroad, provided housing and cooking facilities for the aged and infirm and those who arrived without families.

The refugees named their temporary home "Little Vienna," although the Germans, who were in the majority, insisted on "Little Berlin." Somehow in their crowded environs they found space for roof gardens, cafes and coffee shops. These were poor imitations of those they had left behind but they were places to which they could escape to read newspapers, meet friends, exchange news and ideas, and try for a few hours to recapture some of what they had lost.

European-style shops sprang up along the streets and lanes: one could buy everything from a Viennese pastry to a glass of pure water costing only a penny. Tailors abounded, copying with skill the latest styles and one could find hand-knit sweaters, chic hats and handmade toys, all cleverly crafted from the remnants of former abundance. Sadly, for sale also were priceless antiques, jewelry, cameras, family treasures carried halfway around the world only to be sold piece by piece to eke out yet one more day's existence.

In mid-1945 the danger of Allied air raids was added to lives already tormented by debilitating hunger and disease. Only a month before the end of the war an American bombload intended for the Japanese headquarters went astray and killed a large number of Chinese along with 34 Jewish refugees. That was followed a few weeks later by rumors that the Japanese had surrendered. The refugees hardly dared to dream that their suffering might end, but that day finally came on the 22nd of August 1945. Suddenly it was all over.

The Jewish refugees had suffered much and lost much but they had survived. Shanghai had provided them a place of refuge. Only after the war ended did they learn that this Chinese city had saved them from what befell the families they left behind them in Europe: the Holocaust.

KEEPING FIT IN SHANGHAI

There is no excuse for you to go to pot in Shanghai these days. New recreational facilities keep springing up, the very latest being a stable in Shanghai's suburbs that offers thoroughbred horses for riding, or so we hear (but this may involve a club membership, so check it out).

If your taste is not quite that refined, if you are more of the beer and bowling type, then there is that too. The Chinese have taken to the sport with a passion, and there are now over 1,000 bowling alleys in Shanghai. It has suddenly become a la mode for local young people to take dates bowling rather than to the cinema (we have no idea how the dates feel about this). You will find the facilities up to Western standards; indeed, most were imported from the West. This won't last for long, however; a Chinese company has now entered the market and hopes to outfit 5,000 bowling alleys this year. We can safely say that you really don't need to worry about finding a place to hit the pins.

For pub crawlers there is a Shanghai Darts League that meets every Tuesday in various pubs around town. You can join the team of the pub of your choice. There are also pool tournaments every Monday night, but advance registration is required. (Can we ethically call these sports means to keep fit?) For all sport activities see the What's On column in the monthly *Shanghai Talk*, which provides contact points and telephone numbers.

Tennis courts are a little harder to find, but most of the major hotels have at least

one. There are also several Chinese sports centers that have multiple courts as well as offer lessons but they are pretty heavily booked and you may have to book in advance. Find an expat tennis buff and he or she will be able to tell you where to find the best and least crowded courts. Some of the major hotels also have squash courts.

All the major hotels have fitness centers with all the latest exercise and weight-lifting machines, saunas, anything you need for the complete regime. Body-building has caught on even in China and there are some gyms that specialize in this exotica. These as well as some newly-built sports clubs usually have swimming pools, although they may not be large enough for the dedicated swimmer who wants to do long laps. You can always swim in the Huangpu River; there are swimming platforms down river for those who can keep their heads above water.

If you are a golfer you are really in luck; there are currently numerous golf courses within a 25-mile radius of Shanghai and even more coming on line in the near future. There are also two lighted driving ranges with putting greens on the road to Qingpu and only a few miles beyond the airport. Although most golf clubs prefer that you join — and at rather stiff membership fees of course — at some it is possible nonetheless to pay and play on a daily basis. The newer courses are the most eager to attract customers and are more liberal in this respect. Just ask any Japanese you meet and he will most certainly be able to fill you in on the details; they are the heaviest investors in, and supporters of, the golfing industry here.

The famous, or infamous, Hash House Harriers have a very large and active Shanghai chapter and the location of their runs, every Sunday at 3:00 P.M., is listed in the weekly expat newspapers. There are also pick-up soccer, football, basketball, volleyball, baseball and other ball games, usually announced in the same paper or by word of mouth. (Jocks all over the world seem to have a way of finding each other.) You might want to just wander over to the Jing An Ballgames Hall at 681 Weihai Lu and see who and what is playing.

In sum almost any sporting opportunities found in the West can also be found, albeit sometimes in more limited form, in Shanghai. Rollerblades have made a recent appearance and with the closing of Nanjing Dong Lu near the Bund on Saturdays and Sundays there is even a fairly open and level area for rollerblading or skateboarding. Venice Beach this is not, but if you really crave getting back to the blades or the board you'll now find some space to do so. So sophisticated is Shanghai that you can now also work off your frustrations by battling it out with Laser Tag or Paintball, both of which have their own "shooting arenas" in Shanghai.

Now, sports fans, I mean has Shanghai become The Big Time or what?

We must not leave this subject without at least mentioning the two traditional Chinese forms of exercise that are becoming increasingly popular in the west: *tai ji chuan* and *qi gong*. These are systems of slow movement and breathing exercises which the Chinese swear by as the way to better health. You can join the thousands of groups which exercise all over the city every morning, or you can pay for a private tutor (or "master") until you yourself have mastered the art. (One Grand Master we know is 96 and still in good health, which speaks well for the regimen.)

Now that you are in the country which is the home of both these traditional exercises and of Chinese traditional medicine there is no excuse for your not keeping fit.

LEAVING TOWN

One of the things that will keep you sane in Shanghai is occasionally leaving it. If you or your spouse are employees of Western or joint venture companies then your way is paid out periodically, sometimes as frequently as every three months (lucky you). If you pay for it yourself or if you are really busy here — or if you love Shanghai just too much to leave it — then you may be lucky to get out once a year. (Your author finds that one year is about the outer limit of her tolerance, although she did once last thirteen months before succumbing to Cabin Fever.)

There are lots of ways out: plane and ship for international travel, plane, train and bus for inner-China excursions. Let's start with planes. There are Chinese and international airlines but for local travel you have no choice, you go local. We will share with you a few jokes and anecdotes we have heard from "white knuckle" flyers about Chinese airlines (whose safety record has improved lately, we might add).

For starters the China Travel Press announced that the Chinese airlines have a new chief, a 53-year old ex-vice governor of Jiangxi Province who is described as "a missile expert." He should fit in very nicely. Then there are the catchy campaign slogans suggested (by foreigners, of course) for the Chinese airlines:

— Shortest takeoffs and hottest landings in the industry.
— Take the pressure out of flying.
— Our box lunches are a unique dining experience.
— Every flight is a new adventure.
— Courtesy is the hallmark of our passengers.
— No limit to carry-on luggage.
— Try our Frequent Flyer Program — called "Double Jeopardy."

But seriously folks, the airlines are getting better all the time. Gone are the days, which your author remembers vividly from a memorable flight from Wuhan to Shanghai, when folding chairs were set up in the aisles (would we kid you?). Luckily the aging Russian planes are mostly long gone (many crashed) but you are still advised to check your schedule carefully for the words Antonov, Topolev, Ilyushin or Yak in the column listing the type of plane — and to rethink your departure plans if you find them listed for the flight you are considering.

This being a classless society the trains have no first or second class, just Soft or Hard. Soft class features two slipcovered divans per compartment with two bunks above and a table bedecked with a white doily and atop it a lamp and tea cups. Having only four to a room might seem a great advantage but if three of them are heavy smokers (almost a given in China) then you may want to reconsider. For short trips to popular tourist locations most trains now have coaches with long rows of airline-type seats and there are even Non-Smoking sections (at least in theory) so that solves a lot of problems.

For long trips wooden seats are the norm for the jam-packed Hard class coaches, but cheer up, you will never be able to get into the coaches anyway unless you are adept at climbing through the windows. Many expats prefer the Hard Sleeper class, unless of course they like a modicum of privacy. Hard Sleeper class is a long coach with many bays of six bunks each but with no door shutting them off. The bunks are not really hard; we'd say about the same as those in Soft Sleeper.

The trick with Hard Sleeper is getting the best bunk. The lower one is the most convenient of course but then you offer tempting seating to any and all Chinese passersby who wish to practice their English on you or simply sit and stare at you with friendly amusement. We prefer the middle bunk, where you can lie on your stomach, put the pillow under your chin, and stare out at the passing scenery while ignoring the passing parade (who may not even notice at first that you're a foreigner if you're lucky). The top bunk assures you a bit of privacy, such as it is, but offers no view and is inconvenient. Especially if you have to go to the bathroom occasionally. (But that will soon cease to be a problem once you have gotten a look at the bathrooms; you will probably never go again.)

Hard Sleepers cost about half the price of Soft and as its bunks are open to the corridor at the foot you will always have fresh air — and never lack for of company. You don't get slipcovers but you do get a pillow and a blanket and for the trip to Beijing you can curl up and sleep through most of it. Of course then you would miss the scenery, the fun and the companionship.

There are now fast, clean and efficient, or so they claim, tour busses from Shanghai to Hangzhou, Suzhou, Wuxi, Huangshan and many other nearby tourist destinations. (We have never actually been on one that fits this description, you understand, but then we go to off-beat destinations.) You are best to book all transportation through a travel agent, at least until you crack the code, as they have current information and can supply full details. (And you have someone to blame if it turns out to be a horror show.)

Finally, there are ships that ply the Yangtze and larger ones that sail weekly to Japan and Hong Kong. Some leave from the international pier in Hongkou and some from the Shi Liu Pu pier on the lower Bund. If you are planning to do the Yangtze Three Gorges Cruise before the gorges disappear (better hurry!) you might want to consider flying to Wuhan and starting from there or starting at the top end in Chongqing (it used to be Chungking), and then debarking at Yichang or Wuhan. The reason is that the stretch of the Yangtze downriver is both broad and boring; lots of yellow water and flat fields far off in the distance. Most travelers find it anticlimactic and too time consuming, so they prefer to do their cruising farther upriver and then fly the last leg.

Whatever you choose you will also wish to book these trips through a hotel in Chongqing (who will handle the river portion of the arrangements) or a travel agent. Once we didn't and wound up coming down the Yangtze fifth class (yes, it exists) with the deck passengers and the chickens. These latter and lovable fellow-travelers disappeared one by one each day as we had them for lunch; it nearly made vegetarians of us all.

One final word about flights, this time the international ones. You have the choice of Chinese or international carriers, with the price differentiation — which once made the Chinese ones tempting — gradually disappearing. Fortunately the two-tiered price system, which formerly differentiated between tickets bought by foreigners and by Chinese, has now been abolished. As you might expect, this was done by raising the Chinese ticket prices rather than by lowering those of the foreigners.

For your convenience we list here the major carriers that fly out of Shanghai. If you wish to depart on an international flight from Beijing you have slightly more hassle but many more choices, especially to Europe. Most major European carriers have once-a-week direct flights from Beijing. This is a very fluid market at present, so you will want to check out all your options with your friendly travel agent.

Air China	TEL: 6247-5953
Canadian Airlines	TEL: 6415-3091
China Eastern Airlines	TEL: 6253-5953
China Eastern International	TEL: 6253-2255
Dragon Air	TEL: 6279-8099
Finnair	TEL: 6512-7180/1
Japanese Air Line	TEL: 6472-3000
Northwest Airlines	TEL: 6279-8088
Scandinavian Airlines	TEL: 6472-8827
Shanghai Airlines	TEL: 6255-1551
Singapore Airlines	TEL: 6279-8000
Swissair	TEL: 6279-7381/2
Thai Airlines	TEL: 6279-7170
United Airlines	TEL: 6279-8009

About those travel agents. Previously you were confined to the state-run ones, the China International Travel Service (CITS) and China Youth Travel Service (CYTS). Now private travel agencies are springing up. Check the local English-language newspapers or ask your friends for recommendations. (And if you find a really good one please let us know.) Herewith are the official ones:

China International Travel Service (CITS)	33 Zhongshan Dong Yi Lu
CITS Sub-Branch, Individual Travel Dept.	66 Nanjing Dong Lu
China Travel Service, in Overseas China Hotel	104 Nanjing Xi Lu
China Youth Travel Service (CYTS)	3 Shanxi Nan Lu

Moganshan, Shanghai's Hill Station

If you live in Shanghai and plan to be here in summers then you will want to know about a mountain not too far from you, on top of which is a small settlement surrounded by thick bamboo forests. This village is left over from another era. Its villas remain as they were nearly a century ago, villas to which Shanghai's foreigners and rich Chinese fled to escape the heat and diseases of the sweltering city. (We loved the place so much we wrote a book about it called *Near to Heaven* — which it really is.)

This hill resort is called Moganshan and it lies about 120 miles southwest of Shanghai and 25 miles north of Hangzhou. It has provided summer relief to missionaries and to Shanghai's privileged class for nearly a century. Chiang Kai-shek and his wife Song Meiling had a villa there, as did Green Gang boss Du Yuesheng. Although all the houses are of gray stone from local quarries they are of infinite variety, from small rustic cottages to an imposing Gothic mansion on three levels.

Discovered and developed at the turn of the century by Western missionaries, Moganshan gradually became popular not only with missionary families from the surrounding provinces but also with businessmen and their families from Shanghai and Hangzhou. Until a road was built up the mountain all ascent was by sedan chair or for the hardy a five-hour hike (with coolies carrying the luggage of course).

Most of the early vacationers preferred to journey to San Qiao Pu by canal barge. This "Three Bridge Village" is still there and is still the starting point for your ascent to the mountain top by car. The Moganshan Residents Association early in the century

built a docking facility and a rest house there. They also had the concession for the portage coolies; along with the chair bearers they waited at the rest house to carry their customers and accompanying baggage up Mount Mogan.

Now you can easily drive to Moganshan via Hongqiao Road to Qingpu, Pingwan, Huzhou then turn southward to San Qiao Pu, followed by a leisurely drive up the mountain. With luck the whole trip will take about four hours. For those without cars there are trains to Hangzhou and then tourist busses to the mountain top.

Moganshan's old swimming pool is now used as a reservoir and the tennis courts are overgrown but the mountain trails and waterfalls still offer delightful walks and picnic venues. The air is clear and the evenings cool. Where previously most vacationers stayed in their own or group villas now there are numerous hotels and guest houses ranging from the primitive and inexpensive to those of modest Western standard and prices. A larger group could rent a villa, just as in the old days.

You can also rent a suite in Chiang Kai-shek's old villa, which appears to contain the same furniture it did sixty years ago. It has a large semi-circular balcony with a lovely view down over the bamboo groves that are characteristic of Moganshan. An outdoor dance floor and a new disco in a cottage nearby promise even more lively entertainment.

Our favorite entertainment, however, consisted of watching a Chinese invention that we had never seen: a Bug Zapper. This contraption consisted of panes of glass hanging under a light bulb and over a pan of water. The idea is that the bugs, attracted by the bright light, fly into the glass, bump their tiny heads, fall into the water and drown. Wonderful in its simplicity, it must work; the surface of the water was littered with dead bugs.

Most of today's tourists, however, seem to prefer to do what the tourists of the early part of the century did: sit on long porches, read books, take leisurely strolls or strenuous hikes or just rest and enjoy the tranquillity and the beauty of nature. Plans are underway, alas, to "develop" Moganshan into something quite removed from her quiet and leisurely past. Already some old villas have disappeared and glitzy karaoke bars and cafes have taken their place.

This certainly does not portend well for the frazzled urbanite who simply wants to get away from the chaotic city and do nothing — but in a cooler and calmer clime. Let's hope that the developers spare this little corner of China for yet a few more years so that the Shanghainese and Shanghailanders can still savour it in its original delightful form.

NAMES OF SHANGHAI STREETS — OLD AND NEW

It is useful to know that in downtown Shanghai the city-named streets (Nanjing, Beijing, Fuzhou, Hankou, etc.) all run east-west while the province-named ones (Sichuan, Henan, Jiangxi, etc.) all run north-south. In the old days those main east-west streets were called Big Horse Road (Nanking Road), Second Horse Road, Third Horse Road and so on down to Fifth Horse or Canton Road. When you read narratives and novels about old Shanghai (like Vicki Baum's excellent *Shanghai '37*) that use the old names you must wonder what those streets are now called. To help you here's a list of the more popular ones.

FORMER NAME	PRESENT NAME
Amiral Coubert, Rte.	Fumin Lu
Astor Road	Jinshan Lu
Avenue Road	Beijing Xi Lu
Baikal Road	Huiming Lu
"Blood Alley" (Rue Chu Pao-san)	Xikou Lu
Boissezon, Rte. de	Fuxing Xi Lu
Boundary Road	Tianmu Dong Lu
Bourgeat, Rue	Changle Lu
Brenan Road	Changning Lu
Brenier de Montmorand	Madang Lu
Broadway	Daming Lu
Broadway East	Dong Daming Lu
Bubbling Well Road	Nanjing Xi Lu
Bund, The	Zhongshan Dong Yi Lu
Burkhill Road	Fengyang Lu
Canton Road	Guangdong Lu
Cardinal Mercier, Rte.	Maoming Nan Lu
Carter Road	Shimen Er Lu
Chapsal, Rue	Danshui Road
Cohen, Rte.	Gaoan Lu
Columbia Road	Panyu Lu
Conty, Rte.	Jianguo Dong Lu
Consulat, Rue du	Jinling Dong Lu
Corneille, Rue	Gaolan Road
Cohen, Rte.	Gaoan Lu
Dalny Road	Dalian Lu
Delastre, Rte.	Taiyuan Lu
Dixwell Road	Liyang Lu
Doumer, Rte.	Donghu Lu
Dufour, Rte.	Wulumuqi Nan Lu

Edinburgh Road	Jiangsu Lu
Edward VII, Avenue	Yan An Dong Lu
Foch, Avenue (West Section)	Yan An Zhong Lu
Foch, Avenue (East Section)	Jinling Xi Lu
Foochow Road	Fuzhou Lu
Frelupt, Rte.	Jianguo Xi Lu
Ghisi, Rte.	Yueyang Lu
Great Western Road	Yan An Xi Lu
Haig, Avenue	Huashan Lu
Hardoon Road	Tongren Lu
Hart Road	Changde Lu
Honan Road	Henan Zhong Lu
Jessfield Road	Wanhangdu Lu
Jessfield Park	Zhongshan Huayuan
Joffre, Avenue	Huai Hai Zhong Lu
Kiangse Road	Jiangxi Lu
Kiukiang Road	Jiujiang Lu
Kraetzer, Rue	Jinling Zhong Lu
Lafayette, Rue	Fuxing Zhong Lu
Lincoln Avenue	Tianshan Lu
Lorton, Rte	Xiangyang Bei Lu
Love Lane	Wujiang Lu
Marcel Tillot, Rue	Xingang Lu
Magy, Rte.	Wulumuqi Zhong Lu
Massenet, Rue	Sinan Lu
Medhurst Road	Taixing Lu
Montauban, Rue	Sichuan Nan Lu
Mohawk Road	Huangpi Lu
Moliere, Rue	Xiangshan Lu
Moulmein Road	Maoming Bei Lu
Paul Henry, Rue	Xingle Lu
Pere Robert, Rte.	Ruijin Er Lu
Petain, Avenue	Hengshan Lu
Pichon, Rte.	Fenyang Lu
Point Road	Dinghai Lu
Quai de France	Zhongshan Dong Er Lu
Range Road	Wujin Lu
Ratard, Rte.	Julu Lu
Remi, Rte.	Yongkang Lu
Rubicon Road	Hami Lu
Sayzoong, Rte. de	Changshu Lu
Seward Road	Changzhi Dong Lu
Seymour Road	Shanxi Bei Lu
Sieyes, Rte. Herve de	Yongjia Lu
Soeurs, Rte. des	Ruijin Er Lu

Stanislaus Chevalier, Rue	Jianguo Zhong Lu
Tenant de la Tour, Rte.	Xiangyang Nan Lu
Tibet Road	Xizang Lu
Tifeng Road	Wulumuqi Bei Lu
Vallon, Rte.	Nanchang Lu
Wagner, Rue	Ninghai Xi Lu
Ward Road	Changyang Lu
Winling, Rte.	Wanping Lu
Yates Road	Shimen Yi Lu

TRANSPORTATION RATES
1945

TAXI RATES

Twenty minutes (minimum)	CN 600
Thirty minutes	CN 900
One hour	CN 1,800

Each five minutes in excess of the first twenty (20) minutes CN 100.

RICKSHAWS

Fifteen minutes or less	CN 100
Thirty minutes	CN 200
Forty-Five minutes	CN 250

PEDICABS

Ten minutes or less	CN 100
Thirty minutes	CN 400
One hour	CN 800

Drive on the left.

Walk on the right.

Don't be a traffic casualty.

OLD SHANGHAI'S CLUBS

Shanghai in the fall of 1939 was the most exotic and exciting city in China if not the world. World War II had already started in Europe and Jewish refugees were pouring into Shanghai. The Japanese had been in China for eight years and in Singapore the British were busily fortifying their island against them. And what was happening in Shanghai? Business as usual — and the club scene was swinging.

In that troubled year Shanghai had over two hundred active clubs. Every treaty port in China had its clubs but nowhere did they approach the variety and number of Shanghai's. They ran from A to Z, from the Air Defense Club to the Zero Club. The Amateur Dramatic Club (ADC) was one of Shanghai's oldest, operating out of the Lyceum Theatre; the bar in its Green Room was a popular daylight rendezvous not only for ADC members but also for Shanghai's *jeunesse doree*. Incidentally, the Lyceum still stands, having reclaimed its original name, and still serves as a theatre.

There were three country clubs and numerous clubs for the athletically inclined: a jockey club, a paper hunt club, a polo club, a yacht club, a swimming club and a swimming bath club, the Shanghai Football Club and its rival, the Shanghai Football Association, the Shanghai Rugby Union Football Club, to say nothing of a cricket club, a gun club, a rifle club and a clay pigeon club, and of course golf clubs and for the younger set even a junior golf club.

You could join the Shanghai Wheelers (a "social and racing cycle club"), lawn bowls or lawn tennis clubs, badminton or bowling clubs, the Shanghai Reel Club or the Shanghai Rowing Club, whose club house was on Suzhou Creek just behind the British Consulate General. The Union Church just across the street had its own clubs: the Union Church Badminton Club and the Union Church Tennis Club. Most surprising was a Ski and Winter Sports Club. Since Shanghai has no hills and no snow to speak of, one assumes the club's activities took place elsewhere.

Ninety or almost half of Shanghai's clubs were organized by nationality, representing 23 different countries. The city's large Russian émigré population for example was reflected in the eleven clubs and associations with the word "Russia" in the title.

In both power and prestige in the International Settlement the British were the acknowledged elite. They controlled the most prestigious *hongs* (companies) and held the most important offices in the settlement's governing body, the Shanghai Municipal Council or SMC. Their club was the Shanghai Club with its own massive and magnificent building at No. 3 The Bund overlooking the Huangpu River. Its ground floor, once the home of the famous Long Bar, is now a Kentucky Fried Chicken outlet and its upper floors are used by merchant seamen as transient quarters.

In the French Concession there were two French clubs but the prestige lay with the lovely and lively Cercle Sportif Francais. Although it boasted a popular indoor swimming pool and a number of tennis courts its focus was overwhelmingly social. Its spectacular white verandahed club house still dazzles us today as part of the Garden Hotel, Shanghai's most luxurious.

The Americans were represented by a slightly less elegant white columned building a few blocks from the Bund, one in what contemporary newspapers liked to call the "American Georgian colonial style." It housed the American Chamber of Commerce and the LaSalle Extension University in addition to the usual club house amenities. The building still stands on Fuzhou Lu (and when last seen was empty).

The country clubs and golf clubs were founded less along national lines with the Columbia Country Club, theoretically American, being one of the more popular with Shanghailanders of all nationalities. Located conveniently nearby was a riding school run by former White Russian cavalry officers. The school is long gone but the main club house of the country club still survives, now part of a pharmaceutical research institute. The main club house contains their offices, the squash court their bottling plant and the green sward a truck parking lot. The old arcaded swimming pool appears to be still in use although swimmers must now share it with frogs and fish.

What became then of the scores of other clubs? When World War II came to Shanghai the Japanese closed them all down, interning members of the Allied nations. In the post-war period some had a half-hearted revival, supported by the foreigners who stayed on. These soon found, however, that their role in New China had changed. The foreigners were now less wealthy and privileged and somehow it just wasn't as much fun anymore. Gradually the clubs closed their doors and by 1950 most of their members had left, or were preparing to leave. The club scene and the club spirit left with them. All the elegant old buildings soon acquired new tenants and began their slow decline.

In today's vibrant — and again foreigner-filled — Shanghai, clubs are opening anew but it can never be the same. The old Shanghai, and the life there that made the old club scene possible, is now no more than a distant memory.

PIDGIN ENGLISH

When the foreigners first came to Canton, the only city open to them in the 18th century, they found the study of the Chinese language "irksome, tedious, and unsuited for the conduct of foreign business affairs." They were delighted to find that the Chinese were eager to learn English, anyway a sort of English, which was called "Pidgin," that word being the Chinese attempt to pronounce "business."

To be understood by the English-speaking business community the Chinese learned to string together — in the Chinese fashion — a series of several hundred words, including some Chinese and many borrowed from Malay, Hindustani, Portuguese, and other languages. All were given a uniquely Chinese pronunciation.

Since they could not pronounce some English sounds the Chinese arrived at some strange mutations such as "bobbery" for "bother" and "blong" for "belong," which was used in place of the verb "to be." Since the Chinese language has hundreds of "classifiers" or particles used in front of nouns, for which English has no equivalent, the word "piecee" was substituted for all. This leads to such interesting phrases as that once addressed to your author by an elderly Chinese gentleman she met while walking her brace of dachshunds: "Missi have two piecee dog." You can have "one piecee man" or "six piecee dish" or any combination thereof — and it really saves a lot of trouble.

How would a Chinese say that he did not understand the foreigner? "My no savvy he what-thing talkee; he house blong street other side."

You can't get any more logical than that. We have even incorporated into our English vocabulary some Pidgin: "Typhoon" from the Pidgin word for storm, "da feng" (big wind), and "savvy," Pidgin for "to know," corrupted from the Spanish word "sabe."

Incidentally, at the writing of this book in 1997 the author knows only one person in Shanghai, the old amah of a Russian countess, who still speaks Pidgin. To hear her rattle along in it is pure delight; it transports you back to another era.

Rather than give you a long list of Pidgin words we will tell you a few Chinese jokes and stories in Pidgin and let you figure out the meanings for yourselves.

Can do?

****

The cook asked the visitor what he desired for dinner. Duck was chosen but at that time, while ordinary duck was available, it was the particular season for wild duck. So the cook said, "Missi, my tinkee more better hab flyaway duck today. Can catchee walkee-walkee duck any time."

****

A coolie who was thrown off a horse, on arising from the ground said, "My wanchee go topside he; he wanchee go topside my."

****

A houseboat owner had no cat, but each month the same item appeared on the accounts: "cat chow five dollar." He finally sent for his No. 1 Boy. "What thing every month blong five dollar cat chow? My no wanchee see any more cat chow five dollar."

The next month there was still no cat on board — but the account book now read: "Cat chow five dollar. One piecee cat ten dollar."

****

The Hall Porter at the Shanghai Club answers the phone.
Female Voice: "That blong Hall Porter? Well, my wanchee savvy, s'pose my husband have got, no got?"
Hall Porter: "No, missy, husband no got."
Female Voice: "How fashion you savvy no got, s'pose my no talkee name?"
Hall Porter: "Maskee name, missy, any husband no got this side anytime."

Advice on Use of Pidgin, circa 1945:

At one time Shanghai used quite a lot of Pidgin English. Don't use it nowadays unless plain English fails altogether. The Portuguese, among the earliest of all the traders in the far East, contributed "Compradore"—a purchasing agent, from "compra", "to buy," "Joss" for God, from "Dios", "Junk" from "Chueng".

There	That side
Here	This side
Do you understand?	Savvy?
I don't understand.	Me no savvy.
Where is it?	What side?
Where is that from?	What side catchee?
I don't know.	Me no savvy.
Wait a bit.	Man, Man.
Be quick.	Auso.
Come at once.	Chop, chop.
Never mind.	Maskee.
Can you do this for me?	Can do?
Go upstairs.	Go topside.
Go downstairs.	Go bottomside.
I will pay you later.	Bime bye makee pay.
I want it like that.	Wanchee all same that.
Get me a rickshaw.	Catchee me one piece rickshaw.
Get me the laundry man.	Catchee me one piece washman.

QUICK LANGUAGE LESSON - ALL YOU'VE EVER WANTED TO SAY IN TEN WORDS OR LESS

One of the first things you will want to do when you get to Shanghai is to start language lessons. Without a smattering of Chinese (or *Putonghua* as they call it here) you are really up a creek. We are going to get you started with ten words and are not going to trouble you with those tricky tones (which you would forget anyway). Using the old Point and Pay system plus these ten words, assorted gestures and great dramatic acting skill you just may be able to get your message across. Good luck!

1. WO (pronounced WUH) = I or ME. (Add a MEN to it and it becomes WOMEN, pronounced WUH-MEN = WE or US, see?) The tone is low to rising and if you point to your nose with your index finger when you say it then you don't even need to know that.

2. NI (pronounced like your KNEE) = YOU. (Add a MEN to it and it becomes NI-MEN, pronounced KNEE-MEN = YOU ALL, plural). Now wasn't that easy?

3. TA (pronounced TAH) = HE or SHE or IT, no gender distinction made. Which is why Chinese speakers of very basic English often call men SHE and women HE and so on; to them it makes no difference. (Add a MEN to it and it becomes TAMEN, pronounced TAH-MEN = THEY, as you should have guessed by now.)

AND, if you add a DE, pronounced DUH, to WO, NI, TA — or to WOMEN, NIMEN or TAMEN, like WOMENDE, NIMENDE, TAMENDE — you get neat adjectives: MY, YOUR, HIS, HER, ITS or, for the latter, OUR, YOUR, THEIR. Now who said Chinese was hard? (Its grammar is that simple, trust us.)

4. BU and SHI (pronounced BOO and SHER) = NO and YES. (We did them in that order because you will definitely hear NO more often than you hear YES here.) Grammar Alert! We just told you there was no grammar worth worrying about? We lied. If this BU (or BOOBOO as we lovingly call it) occurred in the PAST, it becomes MEI, pronounced like MAY, the fifth month. Which logically leads us to the most useful and often-used phrase in China:

5. MEIYOU (pronounced like the first half of MAYONNAISE) = NOT HAVE, NOT SEEN, NOT LIKELY, NOT ON MY WATCH, PLEASE GO AWAY, etc. You get the picture. It is a negative, a put-off or a put-down or simply the answer to most of your questions in China regarding objects, as in, "Pardon me, but do you have any....?" — but before you finish comes "MEIYOU!" (Your author once asked an English-speaking grocery clerk if the store carried mayonnaise. The answer was, of course: MEIYOU MAYO!)

6. YOU (pronounced like YO-YO, starting low) = HAVE.
You're only half way through and already you can make sentences. You simply use

WO YOU (WUH YO) and point to an object, and voila!

WO YOU + point to RMB notes	I have money.
WO YOU + point to your husband	I have a man.
WO YOU + wince in pain + point to the spot	= I have a pain in the _____.

This does, alas, limit your conversation to things you can point to but we will get to the intangibles later. Much later. (Your author is still working on intangibles.)

7. YAO (rhymes with WOW, or like someone stepped on your foot, starting high, YAO!) = WANT, DESIRE. Can be very effective with the old Point and Pay System, especially when combined with two little helpers:

8. ZHEIGE and NEIGE (pronounced JAY-GUH and NAY-GUH) = THIS AND THAT. With these, and a finger to point with, you now have the equipment for a whole range of sparkling sentences:

WO YAO ZHEIGE, WO BU YAO NEIGE	I want this one, not that one.
WO YAO ZHEIGE ZHEIGE ZHEIGE ZHEIGE ZHEIGE	I want all five of them!

You are now also equipped with snappy come-backs for those "antique" and trinket sellers who pester you on the street: WO BU YAO (WUH BOO YOW)!

9. QING and XIEXIE (pronounced CHING and SHAY-SHAY) = PLEASE and THANK YOU. Use the first at the beginning of the sentence and the last at the end, use them both frequently and sweetly, and you will be considered a polite and well-spoken foreigner. We lumped these together so that we could save tenth place for the indispensable and immortal:

10. SUANLE (pronounced SWAN-LUH) = FORGET IT. You don't understand my flawless Chinese, my dramatic acting ability, my deft finger-pointing, my earnest efforts at communications, you turkey?

Then SUANLE!

****

Now who ever said Chinese was hard? You should now be able to handle your major interactions with ease. Be a good student, write out a little vocabulary card like the one at right, stick it on your makeup (or shaving) mirror until it is stuck in your mind, and off you go.

Have Fun!

main gate on Yan An Xi Lu. Although badly worn by the excessive activity within its walls Marble Hall is still an impressive building — about as near to a "palace" as you can find in this town. The Chinese named it well.

THE MARSHALL HOUSE (160 Taiyuan Lu)

This was — and still is — one of the most splendid mansions in the old French Concession. It boasts an impressive interior area of 12,680 square meters (nearly 40,000 square feet). A French nobleman built it in 1920 and lived in it until the second world war. From 1945 to 1949 it was the home of General George Marshall, who served as the chief mediator between Chiang Kai-shek and Mao Zedong when he was attempting to negotiate a truce in which Mao would rule the North and Chiang the South of China. As noted in history these negotiations were not successful. From 1949 until her arrest in 1976 the Marshall House was one of the many residences of Mme. Mao, better known as Jiang Qing, formerly a minor actress in Shanghai.

The magnificent mansarded mansion is fortunately now open to the public. It is a hotel whose seven bedrooms and suites as well as its large reception rooms and garden can be rented.

THE MOLLER HOUSE (Shanxi Lu at Yan An Xi Lu)

This faux-Gothic pile is a real eye-catcher with its roof line of towers and spires and pinnacles and every conceivable architectural ornamentation. It is one of Shanghai's most colorful Western dwellings and has spawned all sorts of stories to match it flamboyant appearance. The most persistent is that the owner's daughter dreamed of this house one night, sketched it for her father the next day, and he then proceeded to build it. We contacted the daughter, who also debunked this story.

Another story may be nearer the truth: that the owner, a rich Swedish shipping magnate named Moller, was told by a fortune teller that he should not complete the house; if he did so, something terrible would befall him. He ignored this advice and completed his mansion. The Communist government then came in, Mr. Moller was forced to abandon his home and leave Shanghai, and he was killed in a plane crash shortly thereafter.

He left behind a wonderfully eccentric mansion, its vast rooms paneled in dark,

richly-carved wood and abounding in stained glass ornamentation. Unfortunately it is not possible to view the mansion's interior, as the building now the headquarters of the Communist Youth League and is not open to the public.

WO (WUH)	I, me
WODE (WUHDUH)	mine
WOMEN (WUHMEN)	we, us
WOMENDE (WUHMENDUH)	our
NI (KNEE)	you
NIDE (KNEEDUH)	your
NIMEN (KNEEMEN)	you all, you (plural)
NIMENDE (KNEEMENDUH)	your (plural)
TA (TAH)	he, she, it, him, her
TADE (TAHDUH)	his, her, its
TAMEN (TAHMEN)	they, them
TAMENDE (TAHMENDUH)	their, theirs
BU (BOO)	no
YOU (YO)	have
MEIYOU (MAYO)	no, no have
SHI (SHER)	yes
YAO (YOW)	want
ZHEIGE and NEIGE (JAY-GUH and NAY-GUH)	this and that
QING (CHING)	please
XIEXIE (SHAYSHAY)	thank you.

OK, then SUANLE (SWAN-LUH)!

RECREATIONAL SHOPPING, OR COLLECTING IN CHINA — THE GREAT GAME

"Shopping therefore actually became a stimulating exercise in the abstract possibilities of shape and volume, of geometry. One always came back from such expeditions enlightened...

"As I had about me so much beauty constantly giving me new enjoyment, I continued perfecting my 'scholar's household,' learning daily of further objects, large or small, unknown and charming. Always I tried to acquire one excellent example. The process was effortless, specimens would appear as of themselves, and the whole thing became an absorbing game."

George N. Kates, writing about the
1930's in **The Years That Were Fat**.

Sixty years after the noted Sinophile and collector George N. Kates wrote those words we long-time residents of China are still having our "enlightened expeditions" into that fascinating world, the China of yesteryear. Shopping for antiques in China is no less seductive today than it was then for George Kates. It is a truly absorbing game, the only game in town, the Great Game.

The first adventure is the markets. We are not talking about those set up to capture the souvenir-seeking tourist trade but ones specializing in the *dongxi* of yesteryear. (*Dongxi* literally means "East West" and is the catch-all phrase in China for "thing.") In Shanghai there are five tiers of antique markets, depending on the size of your purse and the amount of time you have to spend in your quest for *dongxi*.

At the top end of the scale are the legal antique stores, where purchases are "sealed" (literally, with a cinnabar colored wax seal) and thus exportable without further ado. The stores are clean, calm, air- conditioned or heated and the customer pays for this comfort. The prices are fixed (and always high) with no bargaining sanctioned. Any sources below this level provide no seals and you're on your own when it comes to getting your purchases out of China.

Next down the scale is the Dongtai Lu market, four blocks full of small white booths in which the dealers' permits are displayed, indicating that the market is at least semi-legitimate. Because of space limitations the items here are all of a portable nature. It is the best bet for porcelains, even though the first asking prices are stratospheric. You just bargain them down to a reasonable level.

The third tier is the "commission shops" where families bring their larger possessions to be sold on commission. These primarily deal in household items, most of little value. Occasionally, however, you find a real treasure languishing among the common odds and ends. In these shops bargaining is the rule.

The fourth tier is your "horse trading" market, currently located on Fuyou Lu in

Old Town. It is open on Saturdays but it is on Sunday mornings that the quiet little street, and the alleys that radiate off it, becomes a bazaar. The street is lined with dealers who have staked out their claims to the better locations before dawn — when the local dealers come to the market to snap up the good stuff for their shops.

The offerings are spread out before you, mostly on a cloth laid right on the ground, sometimes on a table, always in great profusion. They range from ordinary and much-worn objects of everyday use to real and purported antiques of every sort. Incidentally, we once asked a porcelain evaluator of a major English auction house if she had ever seen any Ming or Qing Dynasty pieces here that she thought were genuine. Her answer was, without hesitation, "No."

Some dealers specialize in baskets, boxes and buckets, some in shoes for bound feet, some in porcelain, some in snuff bottles, some in jade, some with almost any category you can think of, everything all jumbled together. It is with the latter that you can sometimes find a jewel among the chaff.

In inclement weather the traders operate under tarpaulins, giving a tent-city effect to the street; because of the lack of customers they bargain better on those days but then the number of dealers is less.

The street's entire clientele — which sometimes seems to be half of Shanghai — crams into the virtually impassable thoroughfares, stopping to gawk at each display of offerings. People on bicycles and vendors pushing carts also try to make their way through the immovable mass, shouting *wei wei* ("make way," "watch out"). You are in constant danger of being toppled over into a merchant's display (and having to buy everything you break). The scene is not for the claustrophobic.

The crowd is primarily Chinese; after all there are thirteen million of them and only a handful of us. In looking down the street into a sea of coal black hair you can easily spot Westerners, partially because they are often taller and fairer but mostly because there will be a little clot of people formed around each of them, watching in utter fascination as they contemplate making a purchase.

This is only at the beginning of the drama, and the better you are at bargaining the more vast and appreciative will be your audience, often even taking your side against the dealer. Sometimes little old ladies or gentlemen, speaking the perfect English learned in some missionary school a half a century ago, will come up quietly behind you and whisper in your ear, "it's new" or "watch out, it's broken!" and then quickly slide away into the crowd.

Although you will never outfox any Chinese in a bargaining session your efforts will often yield an almost even match of wills; the dealer has the item you covet but you, after all, have the money. A devastating moment occasionally occurs when a dealer asks fifty, you respond with an insulting "five" as you don't much want the object — and he immediately says *hao* (good) and you're stuck with the purchase. (If you make an offer then you must buy the item if the dealer meets it; we own a particularly repulsive rattan peacock for this very reason.)

The only words of Chinese you really need to know for bargaining are *tai guile* (pronounced "tigh gway-luh" and meaning "too expensive"). If you can't master that there are still other ways to convey the idea. We personally go for the pained expression as we clutch the heart and reel backwards, but there are other effective ploys. You can shake your head, sigh deeply and walk slowly away; if your offer is in the ballpark the dealer will call out to you, motion you back and try to renew the bargaining session. If he is really hooked he will chase after you with the object in hand — and you've won!

If you are not up to the market scene there is still a fifth and final alternative: private dealers. As we understand Chinese law it may be illegal for them to sell genuine antiques to foreigners but it is not illegal for foreigners to buy them. Any illegality on the foreigners' part lies in trying to export an item that is more than 150 years old without the bill of sale and a proper seal affixed by the Antiquities Bureau.

The most fun here lies in going to the dealers' homes (they will gladly come to yours but there is the problem of their lugging all those heavy items). Some of our most exciting evenings in Shanghai were spent following a shadowy figure into a dark alley, seeing a light through the crack of a door ahead, where an ominous figure lurked, having that door slowly open — to your doom? No, to the whole family, down to the toothless granny, smiling broadly and awaiting your arrival.

What can you buy in the markets, alleys, lanes, streets, shops, stores, private homes of Shanghai? Everything. We never cease to be amazed at the fresh items that constantly show up. You spot an object that you have never seen before and cannot even identify, you finally learn what it is — and you wonder how you could have lived without it for all these years.

There is such a profusion of things to buy that most people rapidly narrow down their collecting interests to one or two fields, say cricket paraphernalia or *sancun jinlian* (three inch golden lilies) silk shoes for bound feet or baskets or bottles or books — and on and on it goes. This makes subsequent searching much more focused and thus easier. (The problem is to somehow keep from expanding the categories of things to collect.)

Each foray into the markets gives you something new to think about, to research or collect. You come across a small shop that has Chinese opera costumes and props: emperor's robes, elaborate plumed head-dresses, platform shoes to add height to the female actresses singing male roles (in Shaoxing Opera), beards that are fastened over the ears like eyeglasses, to turn the young into old. Yet another new world.

As your familiarity with the city's offerings grows, so does your expertise — along with the list of things you may wish to collect. Then comes your desire to find an even more perfect example of some little *dongxi* you collect. An object you never knew existed yesterday today becomes a near obsession. (We have still to find the whistles that used to be affixed to pigeons to make them shrill as they soared.) Then one day, like the man riding on the tiger — the one painted on all the antique dice cups you find in the markets — you discover that you are hooked on The Great Game.

(Excerpted from the author's unpublished MS. of the same title.)

ANTIQUE STORES

Shanghai Antiques and Curios Store	218-226 Guangdong Lu
Antique Bazaar, Huabao Bldg. Basement	265 Fangbang Lu (in Old Town)
Chong Shin Old Arts and Crafts Store	1297 Huai Hai Zhong Lu
Shanxi Old Wares Store	557 Yan An Xi Lu
(and others too numerous to mention)	

...AND "FREE MARKETS"

Dongtai Lu/Liu He Lu, under the arch at the intersection of Xizang Nan Lu	Every Day (afternoons best)
Fuyou Lu, west of Henan Lu, in Old Town	Every Saturday and Sunday morn

...AND WHAT YOU NEED TO KNOW BEFORE BUYING ANTIQUE FURNITURE

There are two questions you should always ask: No. 1 is: How old is it? The answer invariably is "very old" so forget that one. (If the answer is "Ming Dynasty" forget that one too; how much pre-1644 stuff do you really think is lying around antique stores in Shanghai anyway?)

The second question is: What wood is it? Well, what's the point of asking the question if you can't understand the answer? Here are some of the answers you may get:

hongmu	blackwood (AKA mahogany)	xiangmu	camphor
zimu	catalpa	nanmu	cedar
baimu	cypress (very rare)	wumu	ebony
yumu	elm (most common answer)	huaimu	locust
songmu	pine	hongsong	red pine
zitan	sandlewood	limu	pear
yongmu	poplar (aspen)	youmu	teak
jiemu	burl	hualimu	rosewood

huang hualimu yellow rosewood (This one both scarce and very costly).

There are two schools of antique furniture buyers: those who go for the restored and those "purists" (and the author is one) who want it only in its original condition. The latter does limit you to buying pieces in reasonably good shape but with the former you also have the danger of buying a "hybrid," a piece that is made up of several pieces or — even worse — of new wood, inserted to replace missing pieces. If you are not a purist this does not matter but if you are, it is a no-no.

There are antique furniture warehouses all over the western suburbs, especially in the three "Hongs": Hongqiao Lu, Hongmei Lu and Hongxu Lu. As soon as you are ready to start buying furniture you should inquire of other expats; the warehouses' local customers are primarily foreigners. (These dealers also ship vast amounts overseas — almost invariably including the item you want to buy.) The cavernous buildings are stacked to the ceiling with everything from junk to some very fine pieces, and are priced accordingly. Want to buy a Chinese wedding bed? There are scores of them. A wash-basin stand? There are hundreds. The stock changes daily with new deliveries so if you do not find what you want come back again and again and again. That's what the real collectors do.

S THE SOLAR SEASONS

STARTING DATE	NAME IN ENGLISH	AND CHINESE
February 3-5	Beginning of Spring	立 春
February 18-20	Rain Water	雨 水
March 5-7	Waking of Insects	惊 蛰
March 20-22	Spring Equinox	春 分
April 4-6	Pure Brightness	清 明
April 19-21	Grain Rain	谷 雨
May 5-7	Beginning of Summer	立 夏
May 20-22	Grain Full	小 滿
June 5-7	Grain in Ear	芒 種
June 21-22	Summer Solstice	夏 至
July 6-8	Slight Heat	小 暑
July 22-24	Great Heat	大 暑
August 7-9	Beginning of Autumn	立 秋
August 22-24	Limit of Heat	處 暑
September 7-9	White Dew	白 露
September 22-24	Autumnal Equinox	秋 分
October 8-9	Cold Dew	寒 露
October 23-24	Frost's Descent	露 降
November 7-8	Beginning of Winter	立 冬
November 22-23	Slight Snow	小 雪
December 6-8	Great Snow	大 雪
December 21-23	Winter Solstice	冬 至
January 5-7	Slight Cold	小 寒
January 20-21	Great Cold	大 寒

SOLAR SEASONS —
SOME GASTRONOMIC MILESTONES CONNECTED THERETO

FIFTH MONTH FIRSTS - In the fifth month when the corn (called "jade grain" or *yu mi*) first comes into seed the streets are filled with the shouts of vendors calling "fifth month firsts," and of the extremely tender ones they cry "precious pearl shoots." The way of eating them is the same as for eating peas.

SWEET MELONS - By the last part (21st to 29th or 30th) of the fifth month the sweet melons have already become ripe. The street vendors who shout their wares have every kind, such as "dry golden droppers," "green-skin crushables," "sheep-horn honey," "hami crisps," "wei pulps," and "old man's delight."

AND MORE ABOUT THAT FIFTH MONTH:

An old proverb says: "The first month is good, the fifth month evil." In the olden days the fifth month was commonly called the evil month, during which there were many things to be avoided, such as airing beds or mats in the sun, or repairing or building a house.

THE TOP TWENTY TOURIST SPOTS IN SHANGHAI

1. Site of first National CPC Congress, 76 Xingye Lu
2. Former Residence of Dr. Sun Yat-sen, 7 Xiangshan Lu
3. Former Residence of Premier Zhou Enlai, 73 Sinan Lu
4. Former Residence of Lu Xun, 9 Lane 132, Shanyin Lu
5. Lu Xun Memorial Hall and Tomb, 146 Jiangwan Lu
6. Song Qingling Mausoleum, International Cemetery, off Hongqiao Lu
7. Yu Garden and Cheng Huang Miao (Old City Temple), Old Town
8. Jade Buddha Temple, An Yuan Lu near Jiangning Lu
9. Long Hua Temple and Pagoda, Long Hua Town, Xu Hui District
10. Shanghai Botanical Garden, 1 Bai Se Lu
11. Shanghai Zoo, 2381 Hongqiao Lu
12. Shanghai Museum, Ren Men Da Dao
13. Shanghai Natural History Museum, 260 Yan An Dong Lu
14. Shanghai City History Museum, 1286 Hongqiao Lu

AND WITHIN TWENTY MILES OF SHANGHAI

15. Gu Yi Garden, Zhan Nan Lu, Nan Xiang Town, Jiading County
16. Confucius Temple and Hui Long Pond, Jiading Town
17. Pagoda, Zui Li Bai Pool, southeast of Song Jiang Town
18. Ming Dynasty Gardens, Qingpu Town
19. Dian Shan Lake, west of Zhujiajiao Town, Qingpu County
20. Jin Shan Wei and the East China Sea (fishing fleet, WW-II gun ports)

Uncommon Pleasures for the Common Man — The "Great World"

The "Great World" (*Da Shijie* in Chinese, *Da Siga* in Shanghainese) is hard to miss. At the intersection of Yan An Dong Lu and Xizang Nan Lu, it is the massive building resplendent with wedding cake towers, unfortunately now festooned with neon advertising. To compound this misfortune, the whole building was recently covered in bizarre plastic ivy leaves. (No, we have no idea why.) It was and still is an amusement hall but with much more tame offerings than it once boasted. Here's how it was described in its hey-day in the 1930's by the Hollywood film director Josef von Sternberg in his book *Fun in a Chinese Laundry*:

"On the first floor were gambling tables, singsong girls, magicians, pick-pockets, slot machines, fireworks, bird cages, fans, sticks of incense, acrobats and ginger. One flight up were the restaurants, a dozen different groups of actors, crickets in cages, pimps, midwives, barbers, and earwax extractors.

"The third floor had jugglers, herb medicines, ice-cream parlours, photographers, a new bevy of girls — their high-collared gowns slit to reveal their hips, in case one had passed up the more modest ones below who merely flashed their thighs — and under the heading of novelty, several rows of exposed toilets, their impresarios instructing the amused patrons not to squat but to assume a position more in keeping with the imported plumbing.

"The fourth floor was crowded with shooting galleries, fan-tan tables, roulette wheels, massage benches, acupuncture and moxabustion cabinets, hot-towel counters, dried fish and intestines, and dance platforms served by a horde of music makers competing with each other to see who could drown out the other.

"The fifth floor featured girls whose dresses were slit to the armpits, a stuffed whale, story tellers, peep shows, balloons, masks, a mirror maze, two love-letter booths with scribes who guaranteed results, 'rubber goods' and a temple filled with ferocious gods and joss sticks.

"On the top floor and roof of that house of multiple joys a jumble of tightrope walkers slithered back and forth and there were seesaws, lottery tickets, and marriage brokers. And as I tried to find my way down again, an open space was pointed out to me where hundreds of Chinese, so I was told, after spending their last coppers, had speeded the return to the street below by jumping from the roof..."

That changed radically with the arrival of the Japanese. We have no way of knowing what it was like then but a Chinese writer has given us the following account, published in *Anecdotes of Old Shanghai* in 1985:

"When the Japanese aggressors occupied Shanghai, the 'Rong's Great World' became a 'special amusement' centre where people were brain-washed with ideas of enslavement to benumb their will to fight for the nation. After the victory of the Anti-Japanese War, the U.S. imperialists and the Kuomintang reactionaries used it as a propaganda instrument to whip up an anti-Communist and anti-popular campaign. American movies made in Hollywood on pornography and violence dominated the screen and obscene and superstitious operas flooded the stage. Pick-pockets, swindlers, prostitutes and rascals mixed with the audience with an ax to grind. Traitors and enemy agents of every hue were found spying for information or plotting against people's lives among the artists, staff and audience of the Great World. The Great World was, in fact, a paradise for monsters and demons and a den for enemy agents and traitors camouflaged by beautiful music and graceful dancing. After Liberation the Great World returned to the embrace of the people. The people's government took it over in 1954."

Whatever it was like in the old days, it is still worth a visit today. A foreigner's face will probably be as big an attraction as the amusements themselves, as few foreigners ever go there. In fact we have found in all our conversations not one single old Shanghainese or Shanghailander who will admit to ever having been there, except perhaps once as a child "taken there by my amah." This may even have been true as amahs were notorious for taking their charges, once out of the sight of their mothers, to all sorts of exciting but questionable places.

MEET THE COWBOYS AT THE FOURTH MARINES C L U B

Courtesy

E.T. "JACK" RILEY

VISITORS' ONE DAY TOUR OF SHANGHAI

Drive east on Huai Hai Lu (formerly Avenue Joffre) until it melds into the circular road Ren Min Lu, then follow it clockwise stopping at:

The City God Temple in Old Town (Cheng Huang Miao)

This has recently been Disneyfied so what you see is mostly new. There is, however, still the general flavor of an old Chinese city with its little shops, a Ming-dynasty garden, the old temple of the city god and the tea house reached by the Bridge of Nine Turnings. The area is worth at least a half hour's walk-through although the crowds can sometimes be a bit much.

If time permits continue clockwise completely around the old town on the circular road (Zhong Hua Lu and Ren Min Lu), following what were the city walls, and you will get an idea of the size of the original Chinese city. Some old wooden houses and a tall concrete fire watching tower remain amidst the new construction and there is loads of street life to see.

The Quai de France and The Bund

Proceed from Ren Min Lu to the waterfront. The lower portion was called the Quai de France; at the Yan An Lu intersection it became the Bund. Yan An Lu was formerly Avenue Edward VII, the street (laid over a viaducted creek) that separated the French Concession to the south from the International Settlement north of it. Drive or walk northward; if you do the latter use the elevated waterfront promenade. (See the letter W for a full description of each old structure.)

Hongkou and the North

Hongkou (formerly Hongkew), traditionally the less desirable section of Shanghai, lies to the north of Suzhou Creek. (It is said that a Shanghai girl from south of Suzhou Creek would never marry a man from north of it.) Cross the Garden Bridge and turn right into Dong Daming Lu. This was the former Broadway, notorious as a haunt for sailors and merchant seamen. There were numerous chandlers' shops and cheap bars and bawdy houses. Stop for lunch at the revolving restaurant on top of the Ocean Hotel. It offers great views of the Bund and the Whangpu River with its new Yangpu Bridge; the old Ward Road Jail (still a jail, now called Tilanqiao); and the former ghetto area for World War II's Jewish refugees. It takes over an hour for a complete revolution, so dine leisurely.

Pudong, and the Ring Road Circular Tour

Continue northward and cross over to Pudong on the Yangpu Bridge. You are now entering Shanghai's financial district and the future Wall Street of China. While you marvel at the never-ending construction sites remember that a few years ago this was farmland. You will then recross the Whangpu, this time on the Nanpu Bridge, after having traversed the more industrialized part of Pudong. Back in the West you can exit the elevated ring road at either the Cao Xi Lu exit by the Sheraton Hotel or the Hongqiao Lu exit. If you choose the former you get to see the old Jesuit section of Siccawei (now Xujiahui) with its St. Ignatius Cathedral and old buildings in the Italianate ecclesiastical style which formerly housed orphanages, workshops and even an observatory (which still functions as such). If you exit at Hongqiao Lu you can stop by the Shanghai City History Museum and behind it the cemetery containing the tomb of Song Qingling (Mme. Sun Yat-sen), which also contains over two hundred Western tombstones.

This circle tour will have taken you through the five main areas of Shanghai: The French Concession, the Chinese City, the International Settlement, Hongkou, and the new Pudong Development Zone.

Flying Tigers'

GUIDE TO
SHANGHAI

HEADQUARTERS FOURTEENTH AIR FORCE
SHANGHAI
November, 1945

WAITAN - OR, THE BUND — AND BEYOND

After ignoring the Bund for decades, the Shanghai Government in recent years has again turned its attention to it, even to the extent of stunning nightly illumination of its buildings. They now hope to lease those buildings to the original owners, the foreign builders and tenants of more than half a century ago.

We would like to share with you what we have learned about the origins of these wonderful old buildings. As the numbering generally remains the same it should be easy for you to find and identify them. Start at the south end at Yan An Lu. (The Bund south of that road was called Quai de France and little of historical interest remains.) As the title suggests we will also lead you a bit beyond the Bund. As Shanghai's key landmark, however, the Bund is where we will start.

---------- **THE BUILDINGS OF THE BUND** ----------

No.1   THE ASIATIC PETROLEUM BUILDING, built in 1915, later became THE SHELL BUILDING (also known as THE MCBAIN BUILDING, named after one of its tenants).

No.3   THE SHANGHAI CLUB, built in 1910 for an English club founded in 1864. It was said to have had the longest bar in the world   (33.76 meters or 111.4

feet). A portion remains in the Seaman's Club upstairs; the main bar room now houses a Kentucky Fried Chicken outlet. The building is now the Dong Fang Hotel.

No.4 THE UNION BUILDING, built in 1915, used by the Mercantile Bank of India. There was a side entrance at No. 1 Canton Road.

NOTE: Just back of this building at No. 3 Canton Road, south side, was THE ROBERT DOLLAR BUILDING, used by American President Lines.

No.5 THE NISSHIN KISEN KAISHA (NKK) SHIPPING COMPANY, and at one time a Chinese bank and the Chinese Merchant Shipping Company, plying the China coast and the Yangtze.

No.6 In the early thirties it was the home of THE BRITISH P&O BANKING CORPORATION, later was used as billets for the Russian troops of THE SHANGHAI VOLUNTEER CORPS up until the Japanese invasion.

No.7 THE COMMERCIAL BANK OF CHINA.

No.8 A CHINESE OFFICE BUILDING ("Tong Yok Kung" or "Tung Tzue Shing").

No.9 THE CHINA MERCHANT STEAMSHIP NAVIGATION COMPANY, STATES STEAMSHIP COMPANY, and AMERICAN PIONEER LINES.

No.12 THE HONGKONG AND SHANGHAI BANK, built in 1921 as the largest bank building in the Far East. Under its dome was the RAF Club and its ceiling featured a mosaic of early RAF planes. The building served for years as the Shanghai City Hall and Mayor's office, which has vacated the premises; it is now a bank again but not HK&SH, alas.

No.13 THE CUSTOMS HOUSE, built in 1927. Opposite, on the river, was THE CUSTOMS JETTY, where the customs clearances were done.

NOTE: The former building, built in 1843 in the English Tudor style, was demolished and the old clock, "Big Ching," was put back in the new tower. This legend evolved therefrom: After its installation there were fewer fires in Shanghai so the citizens believed that the chiming confused the God of Fire. When he heard the sound of the bells every quarter hour he thought it was the fire bells and decided that Shanghai had enough fires and he did not have to contribute. During the Cultural Revolution (1966-76) the clockworks were destroyed and replaced by forty loudspeakers which broadcast the anthem to Chairman Mao, "The East is Red." In October 1986 the clockworks were repaired and replaced; regrettably the sound of the bells is so weak that it is drowned out by traffic noise.

No.14 Until 1914 THE GERMAN ASIATIC BANK, then THE BANK OF COMMUNICA-TIONS, located at the corner of Hankou Road, or Horse Road No. 3. Before 1930, behind this building was the old GERMAN POST OFFICE.

No.15 Until 1926 THE RUSSO-ASIATIC BANK, then THE CENTRAL BANK OF CHINA. There used to be sculptured heads just under the eaves but they were chipped off during the Cultural Revolution by Red Guards; their sites are still faintly visible.

No.16 THE BANK OF TAIWAN (Japanese). Behind it on Jiujiang Road were the MITSUBISHI BUILDING and the SUMITOMA BUILDING, both Japanese.

No.17 Home of THE NORTH CHINA DAILY NEWS, the oldest English-language newspaper in China (the building was sometimes called the Old Lady of the Bund). It also housed Insurance Companies on alternate floors, and at the back of the building were the printing presses.

No.18 THE CHARTERED BANK OF INDIA, AUSTRALIA AND CHINA.

No.19 THE PALACE HOTEL, built in 1906 at the corner of China's main thoroughfare, Nanking Road. It was famous for its roof garden, which burned out years ago and was never rebuilt. In August 1937 a bomb fell between the Palace and the Cathay (now Peace) Hotel opposite, killing a few Westerners and many Chinese and blowing out the windows on the ground floor of the hotels.

NORTH OF NANJING LU:

No.20 Built in 1930 by Sir Victor Sassoon, the office portion was called THE SASSOON HOUSE and the remainder THE CATHAY HOTEL. Sassoon, an eligible bachelor, lived in the penthouse and built a nightclub under the roof where he frequently entertained. (He also liked to entertain lavishly at his villa in the English Tudor style on the grounds of what is today the Cypress Hotel on Hongqiao Road.) The building is now the PEACE HOTEL but the current lobby is only about one-third of its original floor space; the rest is occupied by tenant companies and offices who are reluctant to move out.

No.22 Until 1924 the CONCORDIA CLUB (built in 1907 for a German club founded in 1865) was a faux-Gothic style building with two towers. It was pulled down in 1934 and replaced by THE BANK OF CHINA, which still operates there.

No.24 THE YOKOHAMA SPECIE BANK

No.26 THE YANGTZE INSURANCE BUILDING, completed in 1918.

No.27 THE EWO BUILDING, headquarters of the famous and powerful British hong, Jardine Matheson.

No.28 THE GLENN LINE BUILDING, also housing the P&O Shipping Corp. In 1941 the Japanese confiscated the building and gave it to the German Consulate, who used the side entrance at No.2 Peking Road. In 1945 the American Consulate occupied the premises; the American Information Service remained on the ground floor until 1949.

No.29 THE BANQUE DE L'INDOCHINE. Its initials were until recently visible, elegantly etched on one of the frosted glass windows. The building has now been totally gutted by renovators.

No.31 THE NIPPON YUSEN KAISHA (NYK) BUILDING, a steamship company whose ships sailed to the U.S. and Canada (taking 18 days to San Francisco, 21 days to Los Angeles).

No.32 THE BRITISH CONSULATE COMPOUND, including:

No.33 THE BRITISH SUPREME COURT.

No.34 THE CONSUL GENERAL'S RESIDENCE.

No.35 THE BRITISH NAVAL OFFICE.

No.51 THE OFFICE OF WORKS.

There were other officers' residences on the compound, most of which were torn down years ago.

NOTE: Opposite was the PUBLIC PARK, where there was an admission charge equivalent of two cents — which effectively barred the coolies. Originally, all Chinese were excluded, save Chinese amahs with Western babies in hand and ladies' maids with their mistresses.

There was reputedly a sign in the park that read: NO CHINESE OR DOGS ALLOWED. In reality the sign was a long list of rules and prohibitions, among which were picking the flowers, the entry of dogs and, at the end, the entry of Chinese. Those two proscriptions, however, were not, as is frequently claimed, listed contiguously in the manner quoted above.

Just back of the British Consulate and facing on Suzhou Creek was the Union Church, one of the earliest Protestant churches in Shanghai. Its tower is now truncated and its front defaced by additions but you can still see by its form and its gothic windows that it was once a church. Opposite it was the British rowing club; one of its buildings is still there but now altered beyond recognition.

Suzhou Creek is still spanned by the old Garden Bridge. In the early part of the century the northern side of Suzhou Creek to the right of the bridge was called "Consular Row" because four consulates were located there: the American, the German, the Japanese, and the Russian. Only the last building remains, once again in use by the Russians as their Consulate General.

Opposite the Russians was the Astor House, Shanghai's earliest hotel. It still stands, a portion of it being used by the Shanghai stock market. On the other side of the road from it stands the Art Deco Broadway Mansions (now the Shanghai Mansions), once an apartment house and now a hotel. It was sold by the British to the Japanese in 1937. British residents resented this sale, but it turned out to be a wise one as all British property was confiscated by the Japanese in 1941.

"X" MARKS THE SPOT —OR, ALL YOU EVER NEEDED TO KNOW BUT DIDN'T KNOW WHERE TO ASK

MAJOR HOTELS:

Equatorial Hotel	65 Yan An Xi Lu	6248-1688
Garden Hotel Shanghai	58 Maoming Nan Lu	6415-1111
Shanghai Hilton Hotel	250 Huashan Lu	6248-0000
Holiday Inn Crowne Plaza	400 Panyu Lu	6280-8888
Huating Sheraton Hotel	1200 Cao Xi Bei Lu	6439-5000
Shanghai JC Mandarin Hotel	1225 Nanjing Xi Lu	6279-1888
Jin Jiang Hotel	59 Maoming Nan Lu	6258-2582
New Jing Jiang Tower	161 Changle Lu	6433-4488
Nikko Longbai Hotel	2451 Hongqiao Lu	6268-9111
Peace Hotel (North Bldg.)	20 Nanjing Dong Lu	6321-6888
Radisson International Hotel	1000 Quyang Lu	6542-8000
Hotel Sofitel Hyland	505 Nanjing Dong Lu	6351-5888
New Asia Tomson Hotel	777 Zhangyang Lu, Pudong	5831-8888
Portman Shangri-La Hotel	1376 Nanjing Xi Lu	6279-8888
Westin Taiping Yang Hotel	5 Zun Yi Lu	6275-8888
Shanghai Worldfield Convention Hotel	2106 Hongqiao Lu	6270-3888
Yangtze New World Hotel	2099 Yan An Xi Lu	6275-0000

MAJOR DEPARTMENT STORES

Carrefour Quyang Store	560 Quyang Lu
Friendship Department Store	40 Beijing Dong Lu
Huabao Building	265 Fangbang Lu
Hualian Department Store	635 Nanjing Dong Lu
International Mega Mart (IMM)	7388 Humin Lu
New World Department Store	2 Nanjing Xi Lu
Maison Mode	1312 Huai Hai Zhong Lu
Next Age (Yaohan) Department Store (Ba Bai Ban)	501 Zhangyang Lu, Pudong
No. 1 Department Store	830 Nanjing Dong Lu
No. 2 Novel Department Store	887 Huai Hai Zhong Lu
Printemps Department Store	939 Huai Hai Zhong Lu
Second Market (Shanghai Style Lighting Co.)	3824 Hongmei Bei Lu
Shanghai Orient Shopping Centre	8 Caoxi Bei Lu
Shui Hing Department Store	152 Huai Hai Zhong Lu
Taiping Yang (Pacific) Department Store	932 Hengshan Lu

HONG KONG GROCERY AND DRUG STORES

City Shopping Service Co. and Supermarket	3822 Hongmei Bei Lu
Jessica (in Jin Jiang Hotel Complex)	59 Maoming Nan Lu
Park 'N Shop Stores (4)	Julu Lu & Ruijin Yi Lu
	200 Shunchang Lu
	Gubei New Area
	Renmin Dadao Underground
Watson's Drugstore (in Shanghai Centre)	1376 Nanjing Xi Lu
Watson's Drugstore	787 Huai Hai Zhong Lu
Wellcome Supermarket (in Shanghai Centre)	1376 Nanjing Xi Lu

BOOK STORES

Foreign Language Bookstore	380-390 Fuzhou Lu
Foreign Language Bookstore (branch)	South Gate of Jin Jiang Hotel, 59 Maoming Nan Lu
Old China Hand Reading Room	27 Shaoxing Lu
Shanghai Bookstore	401-411 Fuzhou Lu
Xinhua Bookstore	345 Nanjing Dong Lu

(Most major hotels also have bookshops; see HOTEL listing for addresses)

DENTAL AND MEDICAL FACILITIES IN SHANGHAI

JOINT VENTURES:

Sino-Canadian Dental Center	TEL: 6377-4831, ext. 5276, 6378-9156
Ninth Peoples Hospital	639 Shizao Ju Lu, Main Bldg., 7th floor
Shanghai Ko Sei Dental Clinic	TEL: 6247-6748, 6247-7000
	666 Changle Lu

New Pioneer Medical Center	TEL: 6469-3898
	910 Heng Shan Lu, Ge Ru Bldg., 2nd floor
World Link Medical Center	TEL: 6279-7688
	Shanghai Ctr., 1376 Nanjing Xi Lu,
	Rm. 203

CHINESE:

Huadong Hospital	TEL: 6248-4867, 6248-3180
Foreigners Clinic	257 Yan An Xi Lu
Huashan Hospital	TEL: 6248-3986, 6248-9999
Foreigners' Clinic	12 Wulumuqi Zhong Lu
IMCC in First Peoples Hospital	TEL: 6306-9484, 6324-0090,
	ext. 2101 585 Jiu Long Lu (near Bund)
Int'l Peace Maternity Hospital	TEL: 6438-2452
	929 Heng Shan Lu
Pediatric Hospital Foreigners'	TEL: 6403-7371
Clinic, Shanghai Medical Univ.	183 Feng Lin Lu

MEDICAL FACILITIES IN THE PROVINCES SURROUNDING SHANGHAI

ANHUI: Hefei

| Anhui Provincial Hospital | TEL: (0551) 265-2797 |
| | 17 Lujiang Lu |

JIANGSU: Nanjing

| Jiangsu Provincial Hospital | TEL: (0250) 330-3836 |
| | 300 Guangzhou Lu |

ZHEJIANG: Hangzhou

| Sir Run Run Shaw Hospital | TEL: (0571) 609-0073 |
| | 3 Qing Chun Dong Lu |

CULTURAL OFFERINGS

Shanghai Art Gallery	456 Nanjing Xi Lu
Shanghai Museum	Ren Min Da Dao
Shanghai Natural History Museum	260 Yan An Dong Lu
Shanghai City History Museum	1286 Hongqiao Lu

(Note: There are over a hundred private museums in Shanghai covering a wide range of collectibles. See the illustrated book *Private Collections in Shanghai*, available in local book stores, for further details.)

SIGHTSEEING TOURS

Jing Jiang Tour Bus	Jin Jiang Hotel opposite North Gate,
Runs all day, makes 8 stops	59 Maoming Nan Lu
(buy tickets on bus, RMB 18)	(look for sign or red bus)
Huangpu River Cruise (twice daily,	Cruise Pier, opposite the Bund
morning and afternoon departures)	at Yan An Dong Lu intersection

PUBLIC PARKS

Fuxing Park (formerly the French Park)	105 Yan Dan Lu
Guilin Park	1 Guilin Lu
Hongkou Park	146 Dongjiangwan Lu
Huangpu Park (the Bund at Garden Bridge)	18 Zhongshan Dong Yi Lu
Jing An Park (former Bub. Well Cemetery)	Jing An Lu at Huashan Lu
Renmin Park (formerly the Race Course)	Nanjing Xi Lu at Clock Tower
Xiangyang Park	Huai Hai Lu at Xiangyang Lu
Zhongshan Park (formerly Jessfield Park)	Changning Lu

YESTERYEAR SHANGHAI
— A HISTORICAL POTPOURRI

THE FOREIGN POPULATION OF SHANGHAI

1910	11,497	POSTWAR YEARS:	
1920	23,307	1945	122,708
1930	36,471	1946	65,409
1942	150,931 (incl. stateless persons)	1949 (Nov.)	28,583

(Statistics courtesy of Lynn Pan, Chinese Heritage Center, Singapore.)

****

"The differences between Shanghai and Hong Kong were, as always, most marked, and not only in landscape. Shanghai might be flat, dirty, and crowded but it was vital, teeming with life and energy. Superimposed upon it, so to speak, was an almost Parisian gaiety, in which Europeans of every nationality worked and played together. The arts, both eastern and western, flourished and one could experience every kind of food and company. If there was vice too...at least it was well covered and did not obtrude itself on the lives of ordinary family folk. In comparison Hong Kong seemed like a Victorian English provincial city, its foreign society strictly stratified according to rank in the Government service, in the British armed forces, or in the banks and large commercial firms."

Written by a Shanghailander
— eighty years ago

****

SHOOTING PARTIES

"The most enjoyable entertainment, however, was one of the shooting parties that Shanghai taipans liked to arrange at that time, and that took you out into the country. You left on a slow, heavy houseboat, and went up along one of the many creeks or canals, where pheasant, partridge, quail, and an occasional woodcock hid behind the tall reeds. The excursion up Soochow Creek to a place called Wong Du was quite popular, and you stayed on your houseboat for two or three days and walked across empty cotton fields to do your shooting..."

Written by a taipan in the 1920's

****

BLOOD ALLEY

At the other end of the economic scale was Blood Alley, whose reputation lingers to this day although the street has long since reverted to one of dull and shabby housing with no trace of its former debaucheries. In its hey-day in the 30's, and again after World War II, it was quite a place. Listen to what Ralph Shaw, a British journalist, had to say about it in *Sin City*:

"Blood Alley, or to give it its proper title, Rue Chu Pao-san, was a short street off Avenue Edward VII — a thoroughfare entirely dedicated to wine, women, song and all-night lechery. The only business of Blood Alley was the easy pickings to be had from the drunks, the sailors, soldiers and cosmopolitan civilians, who lurched there in search of the joys to come from the legion of Chinese, Korean, Annamite, Russian, Eurasian, Filipina and Formosan women who worked the district. Here were the Palais Cabaret, the 'Frisco, Mumms, the Crystal, George's Bar, Monk's Brass Rail, the New Ritz, and half a dozen others — opened in the case of the cabarets around 6:00 p.m. daily and closed, depending on the staying power of the customers, any time after 8:30 a.m. the following day..."

It was on this street where the word "shanghaied" originated. The sailors and merchant seamen had such a good time there that they never got back to their ships. Their captains, needing a quorum to set sail, would send some of their tougher men down to Blood Alley. There the drunks would be drugged (if they were not drunk enough), scooped up and brought back to the ship, which would then sail off before they knew what had hit them. The word "to shanghai" thus entered the vocabulary as a synonym for kidnapping, immortalizing the city where it so often happened.

****

Text of a flyer handed out to sailors at the Shanghai Pier by a laundry man in the 1930's:

Dear Sir,

Would you please give me authorization for can get pickup yiur ship's laundry at qyau. We will perform surly and speedy as showed in price list and serve free of charge (no pay) for Captain's, Exact officer's, and other officer's and Chief's would be served at harf price. Relating to your ship's secret we would be blined, no ear and shut the mouth.

Your faithful servant,
Wang

****

CURE FOR SEASICKNESS

"Seasickness may be prevented by drinking the drippings from a bamboo punt-pole mixed with boiling water, or by inserting a lump of burnt mortar from a stove into the hair secretly, or by tracing the character EARTH on the palm of the hand before getting on board the ship."

- From Chinese Sketches, 1876

****

PUBLIC GARDEN SEATS

"A correspondent writes to complain of 'the habit of certain ladies who go early to the Public Gardens and collect about half-a-dozen chairs around them for friends and members of their families who do not arrive with them and frequently do not turn up at all.' He cites an instance that occurred on Monday evening when a gentleman approached an empty chair and asked the leave of a lady seated near it to take it away. 'Instead of vouchsafing him an answer, she seized a satchel which lay beside her and banged it down on the chair in question to intimate that the chair was engaged.' A most reprehensible proceeding.

"We understand that in future only ladies over fifty-five years of age will engage three extra seats; ladies between thirty-five and forty-five may engage two extra seats; ladies between thirty and thirty-five must be content with one, while those under thirty are not to be allowed to reserve any seats at all."

- From a Shanghai newspaper of 1908

****

LIVING COSTS IN SHANGHAI

"Observation and experience have led to the belief that for foreign residents the average cost of living in Shanghai is about the same as for similar living conditions in the cities of the United States. The old days of a free and easy Orient are gone. The cost of food is now at its highest mark on record. The shortage of foreign accommodations has forced rents to a high point. Servants, popularly supposed to be very inexpensive, are cheaper than domestic help in America, but wages are steadily increasing and this, together with the necessity of maintaining several to do the work of one American servant, makes this item one of importance to the householder."

- Written by a Shanghailander
— nearly a hundred years ago

ZODIAC ANIMALS — A CYCLE IN CATHAY

Each lunar year in China is named after an animal, running in twelve year cycles after which they start all over again. People born in that year are supposed to have certain characteristics connected with it. Your Chinese friends will often ask you what your sign is. (This makes it difficult to conceal your age — but you can always hope they think you are twelve years younger.) Last year was the Year of the Rat, supposedly the first animal to heed Buddha's call and thus the first sign of the Chinese zodiac. The cycle goes like this:

ANIMAL	IN PINYIN	YEARS
Rat	shu	1924, 1936, 1948, 1960, 1972, 1984, 1996
Ox	niu	1925, 1937, 1949, 1961, 1973, 1985, 1997
Tiger	hu	1926, 1938, 1950, 1962, 1974, 1986, 1998
Rabbit	tu	1927, 1939, 1951, 1963, 1975, 1987, 1999
Dragon	long	1928, 1940, 1952, 1964, 1976, 1988, 2000
Snake	she	1929, 1941, 1953, 1965, 1977, 1989, 2001
Horse	ma	1930, 1942, 1954, 1966, 1978, 1990, 2002
Goat	yang	1931, 1943, 1955, 1967, 1979, 1991, 2003
Monkey	hou	1932, 1944, 1956, 1968, 1980, 1992, 2004
Rooster	ji	1933, 1945, 1957, 1969, 1981, 1993, 2005
Dog	gou	1934, 1946, 1958, 1970, 1982, 1994, 2006
Pig	zhu	1935, 1947, 1959, 1971, 1983, 1995, 2007

Editor's Note: Shanghai is a fast-changing city; thus all the data and information in this book is subject to change.

The author and photographer of this book have other publications which may be of interest to readers. They include five volumes of their LOST EMPIRES series:

A LAST LOOK - Western Architecture in Old Shanghai

NEAR TO HEAVEN - Western Architecture in China's Old Summer Resorts

GOD AND COUNTRY - Western Religious Architecture in Old China

FAR FROM HOME - Western Architecture in China's Northern Treaty Ports

THE LAST COLONIES - Western Architecture in China's Southern Treaty Ports
(due out in mid-1997)

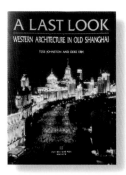

EMIGRANTEN ADRESSBUCH - A replica of a 1939 Shanghai publication which lists Jewish refugees by name, city of origin, profession, and Shanghai address. The authors published this small volume *pro bono* in 1995 to mark the fiftieth anniversary of the end of the Second World War.

In addition, coming out in 1998 is the authors' first volume of a new series, ***Frenchtown - Shanghai***, which will cover in depth selected landmark buildings in the former French Concession of old Shanghai.

Also in the works is a volume of black and white photographs of Shanghai and environs taken by an American photographer for the China Press in the 1920's and 1930's -- and never presented anywhere since. This newly acquired collection of old photographs will offer an invaluable addition to the pictorial record of Shanghai's mid-century history.

The authors continue in their research and in their effort to preserve in photographs and words the Western world of buildings and lifestyle which has for nearly a century added another dimension to China's rich heritage of native architecture and local customs.

The LOST EMPIRES series is available from the authors and publisher, from Hong Kong book stores, and in the book shop of the Shanghai Museum.

Old China Hand Press

P.O. Box 54750
North Point Post Office
Hong Kong

Old China Hand Reading Room

27 Shaoxing Lu
Shanghai 200020

Tess Johnston

TAKE THE
HIGH ROAD TO CHINA
WITH COLLIERS JARDINE
PROPERTY SERVICES

No business today can afford to stay out of China -- howeve
navigating successfully through the world's fastest growing
country is a cultural challenge that must be bridged through
understanding of local business practices and strong on-the
ground experience.

Colliers Jardine has paved a smooth and wide road into Chi
with the broadest national coverage in place - 3 offices loca
in Beijing, Shanghai and Guangzhou, plus 18 management
offices across 7 major cities. Its comprehensive property
services include sales and leasing, tenant representation,
property management, research, professional consultancy
and asset as well as plant and machinery valuation.

All Colliers Jardine's assignments are handled by qualified,
western-trained staff, providing our clients with the assuran
that they are receiving the best professional advice and
assistance to which they are accustomed.

As the pioneer who has marked the trail and guided many
corporations and individuals, Colliers Jardine leads you along
way to fulfill your property requirements in China.

**COLLIERS
JARDINE**

怡 高 物 業 顧 問

34 offices throughout Asia Pacific and 166 other Colliers offices worldw

*For inquiries about Beijing, Shanghai and Guangzhou
please contact our respective offices:*
Beijing - Tel : 86 10 6466 7090   Fax : 86 10 6466 9182
Shanghai - Tel : 86 21 6320 1999   Fax : 86 21 6320 2678
Guangzhou - Tel : 86 20 8669 5176   Fax : 86 20 8669 5602
For all other China inquiries, please contact:
Hong Kong - Tel : 852 2826 9166   Fax : 852 2869 1441

足球场上，两阵对垒，若能掌握因地布策，因时制宜，才是突围取胜的契机。美时正是了解客户在商业竞争上的需要，致力为各行各业的客户创造舒适和高效率的办公环境，体现优质企业形象之要求。

实 事 求 是 的 构 想

十年营销家具经验：服务内地、港、台及澳门地区办公具市场，拥有丰富处理大型工程之知识技术，具处理港七千万元以上的单一工程项目经验，并与客户建立深厚合作关系，成为不少跨国机构及国内大企业的良好伙伴。

健全的网络：在各主要省市设有办事处及拥有共达七千平米展示厅，亦于全国拥有超过四十个分销点，已有逾二名员工，能随时随地为您服务。

货源充裕：在国内拥有六万五千平方米厂房仓库，常备现货值达港币一亿元，故此能应付各项大工程及满足客户速送货之要求。

因 地 制 宜 的 布 局

款式尺码齐全：代理欧陆品牌逾三十多种，风格时尚、功能实用、配件齐全。

高品质要求：全线产品均享有**五年免费保用**，先进产品设计符合人体工程学，物料安全程度达国际水准。

优良顾客服务传统：为客户提供专业咨询和策划，配合电脑绘图设计，大型工程管理及售后服务系统等，由工程构思至落实完成，为客户打点一切。

香港最大上市办公家具公司，领先实力不容置疑：一九九六年集团总营业额达港币十二亿元。

总公司 (852) 2827 6388 • **中国经销商总部** (021) 5881 9119 • **北京** (010) 6615 1347-54 • (021) 6278 8888 • **广州** (020) 8669 9021 • **深圳** (0755) 557 2261, 557 2232 (022) 2330 7976-8 • **珠海** (0756) 811 3889 • **南京** (025) 451 1377 • **成都** (028) 778 9844

美时 LAMEX

力争完美 尽取天时

Above all.....

The Shanghai American Club

Located on the topmost floors of Shanghai Bund International Tower, the Shanghai American Club provides a prestigious venue where both business associations and personal friendships can be nurtured in an atmosphere of sophisticated elegance. Benefiting from spectacular views of the famous Shanghai Bund, the luxurious clubhouse affords discerning members and their families a wide array of business, social and recreational amenities.

Premier Facilities

- American Grill Room
- Fine Chinese Dining
- Formal Lounge with Entertainment
- Banquet & Private Dining Rooms
- Casual Cafe & Lounge
- Delicatessen
- Business Center
- Library & Reading Room
- Fitness Center
- Proshop

Fitness Center

Membership Office -
3rd Floor, Shanghai Bund International Tower,
No. 99 Huangpu Road, Shanghai 200080, People's Republic of China
Tel: (8621) 6393 0517   Fax: (8621) 6393 6766

Hong Kong Marketing Office -
305 Wheelock House, 20 Pedder Street, Central, Hong Kong
e-mail: aci@amerclubil.com
Tel: (852) 2801 6299   Fax: (852) 2526 5033

**SHANGHAI
AMERICAN CLUB**

* Rui Jin Guest House

Avenue Joete
50 Hongkoo Lu

NOTES

NOTES

NOTES

NOTES